Pan Books London and Sydney

00 400 028 256

This revised edition published 1986 by Pan Books Ltd
Cavaye Place, London SW10 9PG
10 9 8 7 6 5 4 3 2 1
© T. W. Smith 1986
ISBN 0 330 50210 7
Photoset by Parker Typesetting Service, Leicester
Printed and bound in Great Britain by
Richard Clay (The Chaucer Press) Ltd, Bungay, Suffolk

Other titles by T. W. Smith in the Brodie's Notes series:
Julius Caesar
A Midsummer Night's Dream
The Tempest
Henry V
The Taming of the Shrew

Contents

Line references in these Notes are to the
Arden Shakespeare: Love's Labour's Lost,
but as references are also given
to particular acts and scenes,
the Notes may be used
with any edition of the play.

Preface

This student revision aid is based on the principle that in any close examination of Shakespeare's plays 'the text's the thing'. Seeing a performance, or listening to a tape or record of a performance, is essential and is in itself a valuable and stimulating experience in understanding and appreciation. However, a real evaluation of Shakespeare's greatness, of his universality and of the nature of his literary and dramatic art, can only be achieved by constant application to the texts of the plays themselves. These revised editions of Brodie's Notes are intended to supplement that process through detailed critical commentary.

The first aim of each book is to fix the whole play in the reader's mind by providing a concise summary of the plot, relating it back, where appropriate, to its source or sources. Subsequently the book provides a summary of each scene, followed by *critical comments*. These may convey its importance in the dramatic structure of the play, creation of atmosphere, indication of character development, significance of figurative language etc, and they will also explain or paraphrase difficult words or phrases and identify meaningful references. At the end of each act revision questions are set to test the student's specific and broad understanding and appreciation of the play.

An extended critical commentary follows this scene by scene analysis. This embraces such major elements as characterization, imagery, the use of blank verse and prose, soliloquies and other aspects of the play which the editor considers need close attention. The paramount aim is to send the reader back to the text. The book concludes with a series of revision questions which require a detailed knowledge of the play; the first of these has notes by the editor of what *might* be included in a written answer. The intention is to stimulate and to guide; the whole emphasis of this commentary is to encourage the student's *involvement* in the play, to develop disciplined critical responses and thus promote personal enrichment through the imaginative experience of our greatest writer.

Graham Handley

Shakespeare and the Elizabethan Playhouse

William Shakespeare was born in Stratford-upon-Avon in 1564, and there are reasons to suppose that he came from a relatively prosperous family. He was probably educated at Stratford Grammar School and, at the age of eighteen, married Anne Hathaway, who was twenty-six. They had three children, a girl born shortly after their marriage, followed by twins in 1585 (the boy died in 1596). It seems likely that Shakespeare left for London shortly after a company of visiting players had visited Stratford in 1585, for by 1592 – according to the jealous testimony of one of his fellow-writers Robert Greene – he was certainly making his way both as actor and dramatist. The theatres were closed because of the plague in 1593; when they reopened Shakespeare worked with the Lord Chamberlain's men, later the King's men, and became a shareholder in each of the two theatres with which he was most closely associated, the Globe and the Blackfriars. He later purchased New Place, a considerable property in his home town of Stratford, to which he retired in 1611; there he entertained his great contemporary Ben Jonson (1572–1637) and the poet Michael Drayton (1563–1631). An astute businessman, Shakespeare lived comfortably in the town until his death in 1616.

This is a very brief outline of the life of our greatest writer, for little more can be said of him with certainty, though the plays – and poems – are living witness to the wisdom, humanity and many-faceted nature of the man. He was both popular and successful as a dramatist, perhaps less so as an actor. He probably began work as a dramatist in the late 1580s, by collaborating with other playwrights and adapting old plays, and by 1598 Francis Meres was paying tribute to his excellence in both comedy and tragedy. His first original play was probably *Love's Labour's Lost* (1590) and while the theatres were closed during the plague he wrote his narrative poems *Venus and Adonis* (1593) and *The Rape of Lucrece* (1594). The sonnets were almost certainly written in the 1590s though not published until 1609; the first 126 are addressed to a young man who was his friend and patron, while the rest are concerned with the 'dark lady'.

The dating of Shakespeare's plays has exercised scholars ever since the publication of the First Folio (1623), which listed them as comedies, histories and tragedies. It seems more important to look at them chronologically as far as possible, in order to trace Shakespeare's considerable development as a dramatist. The first period, say to the middle of the 1590s, included such plays as *Love's Labour's Lost*, *The Comedy of Errors*, *Richard III*, *The Taming of the Shrew*, *Romeo and Juliet* and *Richard II*. These early plays embrace the categories listed in the First Folio, so that Shakespeare the craftsman is evident in his capacity for variety of subject and treatment. The next phase includes *A Midsummer's Night's Dream*, *The Merchant of Venice*, *Henry IV Parts 1 and 2*, *Henry V* and *Much Ado About Nothing*, as well as *Julius Caesar*, *As You Like It* and *Twelfth Night*. These are followed, in the early years of the century, by his great tragic period: *Hamlet*, *Othello*, *King Lear* and *Macbeth*, with *Antony and Cleopatra* and *Coriolanus* belonging to 1607–09. The final phase embraces the romances (1610–13), *Cymbeline*, *The Tempest* and *The Winter's Tale* and the historical play *Henry VIII*.

Each of these revision aids will place the individual text under examination in the chronology of the remarkable dramatic output that spanned twenty years from the early 1590s to about 1613. The practical theatre for which Shakespeare wrote and acted derived from the inn courtyards in which performances had taken place, the few playhouses in his day being modelled on their structure. They were circular or hexagonal in shape, allowing those in the balconies and boxes around the walls full view of the stage. This large stage, which had no scenery, jutted out into the pit, the most extensive part of the theatre, where the poorer people – the 'groundlings' – stood. There was no roof (though the Blackfriars, used from 1608 onwards, was an indoor theatre) and thus bad weather meant no performance. Certain plays were acted at court, and these private performances normally marked some special occasion. Costumes, often rich ones, were used, and music was a common feature, with musicians on or under the stage; this sometimes had additional features, for example a trapdoor to facilitate the entry of a ghost. Women were barred by law from appearing on stage, and all female parts were played by boy actors; this undoubtedly explains the many instances in Shakespeare where a woman has to conceal her identity by disguising

herself as a man, e.g. Rosalind in *As You Like It*, Viola in *Twelfth Night*.

Shakespeare and his contemporaries often adapted their plays from sources in history and literature, extending an incident or a myth or creating a dramatic narrative from known facts. They were always aware of their own audiences, and frequently included topical references, sometimes of a satirical flavour, which would appeal to – and be understood by – the groundlings as well as their wealthier patrons who occupied the boxes. Shakespeare obviously learned much from his fellow dramatists and actors, being on good terms with many of them. Ben Jonson paid generous tribute to him in the lines prefaced to the First Folio of Shakespeare's plays:

Thou art a monument without a tomb,
And art alive still, while thy book doth live
And we have wits to read, and praise to give.

Among his contemporaries were Thomas Kyd (1558–94) and Christopher Marlowe (1564–93). Kyd wrote *The Spanish Tragedy*, the revenge motif here foreshadowing the much more sophisticated treatment evident in *Hamlet*, while Marlowe evolved the 'mighty line' of blank verse, a combination of natural speech and elevated poetry. The quality and variety of Shakespeare's blank verse owes something to the innovatory brilliance of Marlowe but carries the stamp of individuality, richness of association, technical virtuosity and, above all, the genius of imaginative power.

The texts of Shakespeare's plays are still rich sources for scholars, and the editors of these revision aids have used the Arden editions of Shakespeare, which are regarded as preeminent for their scholarly approach. They are strongly recommended for advanced students, but other editions, like The New Penguin Shakespeare, The New Swan, The Signet are all good annotated editions currently available. A reading list of selected reliable works on the play being studied is provided at the end of each commentary and students are advised to turn to these as their interest in the play deepens.

Literary terms used in these notes

The most important is **Euphuism**, from *Euphues, the Anatomy of Wit*
(1579) by John Lyly, a travel romance written in a carefully fabricated
style, which made it fashionable for a time. Some of its features are
adopted (or parodied) in the play:

Frequent **antithesis** (balancing of two opposing expressions in the
same clause or in two parallel sentences): 'a sharp wit match'd with too
blunt a will' (II,1,49).

Overdone **alliteration** (repetition of initial consonants close together),
ridiculed in Holofernes' lines: 'The preyful princess pierc'd and prick'd
a pretty pleasing pricket' (IV,2,55).

Pedantic **allusions** to classical myth: the Nemean lion, dainty Bacchus,
Dictynna (alternative name for Diana).

Artificial **similes**, drawn from nature: 'These thoughts to me were
oaks, to thee *like osiers* bow'd (IV,2,104); 'pecks up wit, *as pigeons peas*
(V,2,315); *'like a crab'* (IV,2,6); or from jewellery: 'His heart, *like an
agate*, with your print impress'd' (II,1,235). An elaborate example is
IV,3,32–3.

Subtle **paradoxes** (apparently self-contradictory statements): 'lose our
oaths to find ourselves' (IV,3,357).

Questions as in a catechism: 'the time when? . . . the place where?'
(I,1,231).

Arrangement of topics in **triads** or groups of three (once practised by
Welsh druids): 'Honey, and milk, and sugar: there is three (sweet
words)' (V,2,231); 'the clown bore it, the fool sent it, and the lady hath
it', followed by a **climax** (IV,3,15–16).

Other terms

Archaism Obsolete word for special effect: 'wight' (man), 'ycleped'
(called).
Dramatic irony The speech or remarks of a character on stage who is
unaware of the true situation: 'What will Berowne say?' (IV,3,142).
Hendiadys Two nouns instead of one noun described by an adjective:
'oaths and gravities' for grave oaths (V,2,760).
Hyperbole Exaggeration for the sake of emphasis or vividness:
'(women's eyes) show, contain, and nourish all the world' (IV,3,349).
The word itself is used in V,2,407.
Metonymy A symbolic reference using an associated word: 'gives the
crutch the *cradle's* infancy' (IV,3,241).
Prolepsis The result is anticipated: 'no woman may approach his *silent*
court' (II,1,24). Cf. also 1.87.

Synecdoche A part represents the whole: 'aged *ears* play truant at his tale' (II,1,74).

Tautology Repetition of the same word or the same idea in different words, sometimes for emphasis, sometimes a defect. Notice the subtle nuances in the repetition of 'pain' (I,1,73), 'want' (IV,3,233), 'sense' (V,2,259). **Pleonasm** is unnecessary repetition: 'both twain' (V,2,429), 'base vulgar' (I,2,45).

Metre

Rhythm (measured movement) in verse or prose is created when a certain arrangement of stressed and unstressed syllables satisfies the ear. The rhythm of each line of verse is defined by its metre: the number and nature of its 'feet'. The two most important metres in English verse are the **iambic** foot of two syllables with the stress on the second, x/, and the **trochaic foot** /x of two syllables with the stress on the first /x. The bulk of our poetry and of Shakespeare's plays is in **iambic pentameters** (five feet). If unrhymed they constitute **blank verse**. The only example in the play of the more lyrical **trochaic metre** is Dumain's poem.

Rhyme (strictly 'rime', mis-spelt through confusion with 'rhythm') is the agreement (sometimes approximate) in sound of the final syllable of two or more lines. Much of Shakespeare's early work is in **rhymed couplets**, with occasional **quatrains,** rhyming *abab;* the dialogue of the four men in IV,3,210–285 is entirely in quatrains; when Berowne responds to the request for serious argument, he reverts to blank verse. Rhyme may mark passages that are lyrical, passionate or very artificial. Costard manages to fit rhymes to some quite unmetrical lines (IV,1,141–9).

Stress variation If the stress fell regularly on the second syllable of each iambic foot the effect would, of course, be very monotonous. In good verse it moves frequently to the first syllable, especially in the first foot: /xx/x/x/x/.

Study is like the heaven's glorious sun.

It is also worth noting that all five stresses in a pentameter are not of equal weight: characteristic of Shakespeare are the changes rung on three major and two minor stresses.

The play
Plot, sources and treatment

Plot

Ferdinand, King of Navarre, a southern neighbour of France, has persuaded three of his courtiers, Berowne, Longaville and Dumain, to join him in a three-year period of study, under certain conditions, the chief of which is abstention from the company of women. When called on to subscribe, two immediately comply, but Berowne first argues the impracticability of his vow, then signs under protest, and finally boasts he will keep it longer than the others. The arrival of a Princess of France, on an embassy and accompanied by a corresponding number of ladies, adds substance to Berowne's objection.

The same condition having been proclaimed within the precincts of the Court, a peasant named Costard has been denounced to the King for keeping company with a dairymaid. The denouncer Armado, a fantastic Spanish knight, temporarily resident, would like her for himself. He is sentenced to a week's fast and handed over to Armado's custody.

The embarrassed King meets the Princess and her suite in a scene in which all four gentlemen are clearly interested in the four ladies. For his part the King, doubtless moved by the Princess's beauty, agrees to a financial settlement favourable to her father, the King of France, but feels compelled, out of regard for his solemn vow, to accommodate his guests not in the palace but in pavilions in the park.

Costard, having been freed by Armado so that he may carry a letter to the dairymaid Jaquenetta, is also entrusted by Berowne, for reasons of secrecy, with *his* missive to Rosaline – with whom, despite his mocking attitude to such matters, he has fallen in love. The peasant's apparent blunder in exchanging the letters gives rise to the main action of the play, which is in Act IV. First he hands Armado's grossly affected letter to Rosaline's mistress, whereupon it is read aloud to general amusement; he then gives Berowne's letter to Jaquenetta, who takes it to the parson and is told to deliver it to the King himself – of all people!

Meanwhile, somewhere else in this spacious park, Berowne,

from his hiding-place, observes the King reading out his love-poem to the Princess and then hiding to observe Longaville reading out *his* love-poem to Maria, then hiding to observe Dumain reading out *his* love-poem to Katharine. Each emerges in turn to confront the one he has observed, until Berowne crowns these successive exposures of hypocrisy with a withering comparison of their weakness with his own invulnerability. His triumph is short-lived, for Costard and Jaquenetta arrive with the tell-tale letter. Unashamedly declaring that they are now a quartet of infatuated oath-breakers, Berowne responds to the King's appeal to him for some way out of their predicament; he justifies their behaviour in a long speech, proving casuistically that 'love fulfils the law'. They then depart, determined to woo their respective ladies and arrange for their entertainment.

In the long final scene the contest is fought and 'lost'. First, the ladies are comparing love-tokens when Boyet (the French lord in attendance, who has done some spying on his own account) warns them that the lovers are approaching, masked and disguised as Russians. On the Princess's suggestion, they exchange tokens, Rosaline posing as the Princess, to whom accordingly the King pays his addresses, while Berowne seeks the company of the Princess. Each of the four pairs has a moment's private conversation before all the men are dismissed, to reappear in their own persons and discover the trick that has been played on them. Berowne's fierce attack on Boyet as a spoilsport is interrupted by the farcical presentation of 'The Nine Worthies', by Armado and the locals, as part of the 'entertainment'. Their well-intentioned but mercilessly criticized efforts are an anticipation of the famous perpetration of 'Pyramus and Thisbe' in *A Midsummer Night's Dream.*

'Pompey' (Costard) having been informed that Jaquenetta has been made pregnant by 'Hector' (Armado), an impending, if ridiculous, duel is brought to a sudden and dramatic stop by the news of the French King's death. The Princess regretfully decides on an instant return to France; however, each lady in turn promises to receive further addresses at the end of the twelvemonth period of mourning, provided this time has been penitentially spent by her lover in good works. The King is to live the life of a hermit (with not even a gay pavilion to accommodate him!), while Berowne, the witty scoffer, is to spend the time visiting bedridden patients too sick to laugh at his jokes.

Sources and treatment

No single work of literature has been found as a direct 'source' of plot or characters in this play, but there is an abundance of scattered allusions undoubtedly drawn from Shakespeare's reading or from contemporary affairs. There have been interesting theories expounded in research theses or learned periodicals; much evidence will have been lost in books or tracts that have vanished long ago, for it was an age of pamphleteering and bitter quarrels between different schools of thought and rival partisans of prominent nobles. Pin-pricking ridicule and savage satire, expressed in uncouth terms, if they could be recovered, would make *Love's Labour's Lost* seem less extravagant! It has some doggerel verse and several atrocious puns which may have been pointed references in the sixteenth century, but are unlikely ever to be satisfactorily explained. For a thorough and interesting account of these problems, the student should consult 'The Topical Context' in Richard David's Introduction to the Arden Edition, (pp. xxxii to xlii).

There has been much research into possible models for the comic characters, who seem such obvious caricatures. **Armado** (his name recalls the 'magnificent Armada') *may* have been Sir Walter Raleigh: whether he suffered from a shortage of shirts or was stingy in rewarding the deserving, we do not know, but Raleigh's love-affair with one of Elizabeth's maids of honour brought him serious trouble. **Holofernes** *may* have been suggested by John Florio, whose translation of Montaigne was widely read, or merely by some recollected schoolmaster; his unusual name was that of a tyrant slain by a Jewish heroine (see the Biblical Apocrypha) and of a tutor in *Gargantua* by the French satirist, Rabelais (d.1553), who took five years to teach his pupil to say his ABC backwards. **Moth** has been linked with Thomas Nashe, writer and pamphleteer who died young at 33; he was short of stature.

The historical parallels are less intriguing. Contemporary events in France would be well known to Shakespeare, but he adapted them to suit his purposes – more freely than he could with similar personages and happenings in English history. The actual record may be briefly summarized:

In 1589, the year after the defeat of the Spanish Armada, which so encouraged the Protestants of Europe in their conflicts with the Catholics, the French King Henry III died at the hands of an assassin and was succeeded by another Henry, the Protestant King of Navarre, his brother-in-law, who soon had a lengthy civil war on his hands. The only royal **Ferdinand** in Navarre was the King of Aragon, who seized most of the country in 1512. At the victory of Ivry, in 1590, one of the new King's marshals was the Duc de Biron, under whom English volunteers were serving. He was a proud and boastful man, whose later resentment at what he regarded as royal ingratitude led him to treason (he supported the Renaissance idea of an ideal republic) and a sensational execution in 1601. Another marshal was the Duc de Longueville. Prominent among the King's enemies, and one who eventually came over to his side, was the Duc de Mayenne. The activities of the Duc de Biron may have inclined our author to give him more prominence in the later version of the play (still later, in 1610, when on a brief embassy to England, he was taken to the Tower by Queen Elizabeth and shown the head of Essex, a recently executed 'rebel', but the hint was not taken). It was a time of plot and counter-plot, of secret letters and paid spies.

Henry III had succeeded two brothers, all three being rather effeminate in an exaggerated Italian fashion (perhaps caricatured in **Boyet**). Navarre was a gallant warrior (note the military terms in the play), but the knowledge that he had had many mistresses would have made the plan to forswear feminine company good for a laugh in London. He had married his Princess (Marguerite) before ascending the throne of Navarre, and she was the sister, not the daughter, of Henry III. This partial parallel is chiefly of interest in that Shakespeare borrowed the names of three real noblemen, while keeping his **Princess** anonymous. One wonders what Elizabeth (for whose reception during her progresses her nobles spent large sums on buildings and furnishings) would have thought of the Princess's accommodation in a pavilion in a park! And what are we to make of a sovereign turned poet who crams his verses into both sides of the sheet, margins included?

Some long-forgotten hit? Most fascinating of many speculations about this play is the suggestion that in the characters of **Berowne** and **Rosaline** Shakespeare was drawing on his relationship with the 'Dark Lady of the Sonnets'.

Text and date

In 1598 appeared the First Quarto of *Love's Labour's Lost*, the first of our author's plays to bear his name on the title-page. Included in the title were the words, 'As it was presented before her Highness this last Christmas', so we can imagine the real courtiers' laughter at the Worthies' prodigious efforts and Moth's uncharacteristic stage fright. Also 'Newly corrected and augmented By W.Shakespeare', which throws a glimmer of light on the discrepancies in the text; whether these alterations were few or numerous, made to the prompt copy or to some vanished quarto, can only be guessed. In some cases there would be an improvement; in others we have contradictions, fragmentary references or incomplete allusions (like that to Katharine's sister in V,2,14). Added to the errors of compositors working to ear, whose lettering was checked with more attention to correct lining and typography than actual meaning, they have kept editors busy.

As the first Elizabeth was a severe critic of the entertainment as well as the accommodation provided for her, one wonders whether the 'augmentations' were made before or after the royal command performance. A nobleman might feel compelled to add a whole wing to his otherwise inadequate mansion; did Shakespeare extend his last scene into a veritable Long Gallery in which Berowne could strut, scold the wretched Moth like an infuriated producer, bandy words with the Princess herself, caricature Boyet and then insult him, play a leading part in baiting the Worthies and, finally, receive his 'sentence' (not one of execution, like his historic counterpart)?

The date of any original version can only be guessed at. In 1593 the public theatres were closed because of an outbreak of bubonic plague (possibly referred to in III,1,196 and V,2,421) when a play like this one could be performed on a private stage. At this period, too, Shakespeare was producing the sonnets and poems to which much of the ideas and diction, not to mention the actual 'sonnets' of the lovers, bears a strong affinity. The First Folio of 1623 has a large number of variations from the Quarto, mostly minor ones. The naming of the characters in the directions is chaotic: some lines, and indeed some speeches, are given to the wrong speakers. The King is Ferdinand in the first scene, then Navarre and afterwards just the King; to cap that, the Princess even becomes the Queen on two occasions; 'Costard' enters, but 'Clown' speaks, and later 'enter Pompey'; Holofernes becomes typecast as the Pedant and Nathaniel as the Curate; Moth fluctuates between Boy and Page; lastly, Armado is quickly and permanently labelled the Braggart.

In three places duplication, probably caused by the compositor or his reader overlooking signs for erasing, has to do with Berowne. In IV,3 the repetition of the line:

From women's eyes this doctrine I derive

at lines 298 and 346 indicates almost certainly in this unnaturally long speech (even for Berowne) that two versions are embodied in it (see Textual Notes to this scene). At V,2,809 his words:

And what to me, my love? and what to me?

are not only a senseless anticipation of Dumain's a few lines below, but so inferior to the real confrontation at line 829:

Studies my lady? Mistress, look on me . . .
Impose some service on me for thy love.

Similar, but more intriguing, is the duologue in II, 1 from line 179:

Lady, I will commend you . . . thanksgiving.

The Folio gives this to Boyet, the Quarto to Berowne. Nearly all editions follow the Quarto, but surely, since Berowne and Rosaline have had one sparring match earlier in the scene (with the dramatic purpose of giving the King time to read the message) and are to indulge in another after the other two pairs have had their turns, this extra sally in between is not only too much, but clumsy stage production. It is undignified for the King to leave unaccompanied by his attendant lords; much more effective than each coming forward in turn is for one after another, when the whole party has left the stage, to steal back for one more look and to learn the name of his particular lady. The intervening dialogue, with which lady does not matter much, is better undertaken by Boyet – it is more characteristic of him, too, as a comparison with his contest with Maria (IV,1,133) will confirm.

No one will ever be quite sure what is meant by 'The party is gone' (V,2,663). Is it a misplaced stage direction or is it dialogue? Is it said by Armado or Costard? Does it refer to a departed Worthy or to a pregnant Jaquenetta? And how on earth could such a condition be blamed on Armado, who has not even succeeded in getting an assignation with her, whereas Costard has been her regular companion? True, with the simple-mindedness of his fellow-countryman Don Quixote, he promises chivalrously to support her for three years (obviously this is what the peasant status of holding the plough must mean). Can his fate (forced marriage) and the contrary fate of the courtiers (postponed marriage) be placed together under the heading of Poetic Justice?

Scene summaries, critical comment, textual notes and revision questions

Act I Scene 1

The King of Navarre calls on three of his courtiers to sign their names after taking oath to keep a compact forbidding them certain pleasures during a three-year course of philosophic study. Longaville and Dumain willingly consent but Berowne, before signing, repeats (for the benefit of the audience) the conditions:

1 To see no women during this period.
2 To fast one day a week and eat only one meal on each of the other days.
3 To sleep no more than three hours a night.

He protests that these are vain conditions, that he has sworn only to study, and that if he *did* swear to the conditions it was in fun. Twisting the King's definition of study as 'getting to know the otherwise unknown' into 'getting to know the forbidden', he professes to agree to:

1 Find a hidden dining place.
2 Meet a woman in secrecy.
3 Break his word without really doing so.

Reproached by the King for being obstructive, Berowne declares that the vainest of all delights to indulge in is poring over books and ruining one's eyesight – better to exercise that eyesight by gazing into women's eyes. The best kind of study is that of the stroller under the starry skies who is quite unable to name the constellations, that secondary form of knowledge acquired from musty books.

Taunted by the others and invited by the King to abandon his part in the enterprise, Berowne refuses to retract his oath and prepares to sign, first reading out two further provisions he finds in the document: that any woman coming near the Court should lose her tongue (a penalty devised by the eager Longaville), and that any man talking to a woman should be put to the maximum shame. Here Berowne reminds the King (who seems to have forgotten) that a French Princess is expected hourly.

The embarrassed King decides at first that the visitors must be received 'out of necessity', an expression which Berowne shrewdly declares will serve as his excuse for any infringement; he signs, boasting that he will keep his oath longer than the others.

For their entertainment they are promised something as good as any paid minstrel: the fantastic use of language by a visiting Spaniard called Armado. At this very moment the constable brings in a peasant called Costard, and a letter from the same Armado explaining in grotesque detail his arrest of Costard for breaking the new law against meeting women. Interrogated by the King, the peasant is sentenced to fast for a week on bread and water and entrusted to Berowne for delivery to the safe-keeping of Armado.

Commentary

The opening lines are an extreme assertion, in typically affected diction, of a philosopher's highest ambition: to be commemorated after death as a famous scholar. This enjoyment is to be gained by the sacrifice of three youthful years of natural pleasures, these being spent instead on devoted study in a state of monkish celibacy – contemplation of the ideal, not experience of real life. It is this decision that leads to all the odd situations and often farcical behaviour in the play.

The proposal, intended to bring everlasting fame to this remote kingdom of Navarre, is made by the King himself, and his courtiers are expected to follow suit. There would seem to have been some preliminary discussion, concluded in verbal oaths; now the King calls on his three fellow students to confirm their corporate undertaking by signing their names on paper. Does he distrust them? Is he selfishly pursuing a personal ambition? These minor matters are swallowed up in the debate maintained by Berowne against the others. While Longaville and Dumain meekly concur, both using the word 'pine' to express their self-denial of all customary enjoyments, Berowne first exposes the absurdity of the scheme, made still more inconvenient by the Princess's visit, and then signs defiantly. His eloquence develops from an ironical conversion of the King's definition of study into a paradox – a tissue of elaborate and far-fetched analogies, illuminating the contrast of the key ideas of 'light' and 'dark' in equally elaborately rhyming couplets and quatrains.

The absent-minded sovereign is prevented by Berowne from impulsively breaking his promise in order to receive the Princess properly; he also omits to indicate the alternative accommodation he provides, at short notice, leaving the audience to create for itself an impression of gaily furnished pavilions pitched in the royal park, with hunting laid on as entertainment.

Armado's letter arouses keen anticipation of the appearance of the highly praised Spanish knight.

Brazen tombs Monuments in church with brass plates recording the achievements of the dead.

disgrace Misfortune (through being out of favour with Fortune).

cormorant Greedy, like the bird of that name.

Th'endeavour of this present breath The efforts of our bodies while still alive.

That honour i.e. the 'fame' of line 1.

bate Blunt.

scythe's keen edge The sharp edge of the scythe, a symbol often carried by Time in the form of an old man.

war against your own affections Strive to overcome natural feelings of love.

late edict The proclamation he has recently made.

strongly stand in force Be strictly observed.

academe Academy, a school of philosophy. From the name of a garden in Athens where Plato taught.

Still and contemplative in living art Meditating in quiet on the art of living.

his own hand may strike his honour down i.e. his signature will be a witness against him; 'him' is understood as antecedent to 'That violates'.

armed Equipped spiritually. Suggested by 'strike' above?

deep Solemn.

keep it i.e. your word (understood).

paunches Stomachs. In modern use only for prominent ones.

pates Heads.

dainty bits Choice morsels of food.

bankrupt Reduce to poverty (contrasting with 'make rich').

Dumain is mortified i.e. I hereby renounce all worldly pleasures. To 'mortify the flesh' meant to make it dead to all desires.

The grosser manner The coarser forms.

thrown upon Gives away to.

baser Than the 'gross world' or than Dumain himself?

all these i.e. his present companions.

say their protestation over Repeat what they have solemnly declared.

dear liege My lord.

in that term During the three years.

enrolled Recorded as an item in a list.

of all the day Throughout the daytime.

all night i.e. in sleeping all night.

make a dark night i.e. sleep.

passed, to pass away Given, to abstain from. A pun on (1) to pass or give an oath, as in 'pass judgement', and (2) to depart from, as in 'let this cup pass from Me'.

an if If. Occurs in several places.

I only swore to study i.e. without the other restrictive conditions.

By yea and nay i.e. without any unnecessary oaths. cf. Matthew 5, 37: 'Let your communication be, "Yea, yea; Nay, nay".'

hid and barred Concealed and barricaded.

from common sense From the limited understanding of the average person (not the present meaning).

study's god-like recompense i.e. the reward of knowing, like the gods, things that are hidden from ordinary mortals.

I will swear to study so i.e. to find out for myself what is hidden from me (by these prohibitions).

to feast i.e. to have more than one meal a day.

from common sense are hid i.e. forbidden to me as a person of only 'common sense' (see above).

break it . . . troth i.e. break my sworn promise without destroying my reputation for honesty.

study's gain The benefit gained from study.

Study knows . . . know i.e. my kind of study is devoted to that which it has not yet found out. Berowne's far-fetched arguments end in a paradox.

stops Impediments.

train Draw (by temptation). The very opposite of the modern use.

with pain purchased . . . pain i.e. (the vainest of all delights is that which,) obtained by hard self-denial, brings pain with it.

falsely blind the eyesight of his look i.e. treacherously deprive him of his physical eyesight (by overstrain). The tautology is simply rendered thus: 'blind the eyes, leaving the reader without eyesight when he looks at a book'. 'Look' is a rhyme-word for 'book'. 'Falsely' is a deliberate paradox with 'truth'.

Light seeking light . . . beguile Playing on four meanings of the word: The understanding (1) in its prolonged search for truth (2) deprives the eyes (3) of their vision (4).

where light in darkness lies i.e. the solution to your problems.

Study me Archaic dative, i.e. study for me or at my request.

a fairer eye i.e. one belonging to the fair sex.

Who dazzling so . . . blinded by Thanks to the elaborate rhyming scheme, Berowne's meaning is itself almost out of sight! Perhaps he means: 'That eye which dazzles the beholder by its beauty shall be the object of his contemplation (to which he pays "heed"), and shed light upon him whom previously it had blinded.' The prose order of the last five words is: 'Who was blinded by it'. 'By' had to rhyme with 'eye' two lines up.

saucy looks Impudent stares at it.

Small i.e. small profit.

continual plodders i.e. those who spend years in mere reading.

base authority Second-hand and therefore inferior knowledge ('base' suggests something illegitimate).

earthly godfathers i.e. astronomers who have assisted in 'baptizing' the stars.

wot not what they are i.e. don't know their names.

nought but fame i.e. reputation for scholarship and nothing else.

every godfather can give a name i.e. every sponsor at baptism can call anything by its name, while ignorant of its (true) nature.

How well he's read . . . reading! i.e. his arguments are based on his own reading. (This line is a paradox, followed by another in the next line, based on a pun.)

Proceeded well . . . good proceeding i.e. took a good degree (a university expression) in order to prevent good actions (like ours).

He weeds the corn i.e. he pulls up the corn (instead of the weeds).

green geese i.e. one-year-olds. 'Breeding' was suggested by 'weeding'. Is this a tilt at the others as youthful simpletons?

Fit in his place and time i.e. Berowne's previous remark ('his' means 'its') is apt for the people addressed and the time when it was made.

In reason nothing There is no reason in it.

Something then in rhyme i.e. if you will not allow me my reason, I will score something by a rhyme (with 'time'). The expression 'without rhyme or reason' survives.

sneaping Nipping (obsolete).

frost The pun is on 'rime' (hoar-frost) and 'rhyme' (for which it is substituted).

first-born infants Early blooms. Perhaps referring to Berowne's attack on them as 'green geese'.

Why should proud summer . . . sing? Why should summer precede spring, contrary to season? In other words: Why give priority to scholarship over love-making?

abortive birth Birth in which nothing is born alive.

new-fangled shows Fresh fashions in flowers. A contemptuous expression – we still use it.

like of Have a liking for.

Climb o'er the house . . . gate i.e. waste much effort acquiring knowledge by shutting yourselves out of the world instead of using direct access.

sit you out i.e. take no further part.

for barbarism i.e.on behalf of the anti-academic side.

that angel knowledge Those delightful studies of yours.

you can say You are able to find words (in their defence).

bide the penance . . . day Endure the punishment of each day of the whole three years.

Marry Exclamation from 'by St Mary!'

Sweet lord Sarcastic.

A dangerous law against gentility In the Folio this line is a continuation of Longaville's remark, meaning perhaps 'a severe decree to keep out well-bred young ladies', but better attributed to Berowne: 'What a frightful threat to the fair sex!'

Aquitaine A once mighty dukedom, reduced at this time to a geographical expression. The references to it and to the Princess's 'bed-ridden father' (Charles VI, d.1422, is the only, and most likely, parallel) are barren clues to any basis in fact.

overshot Gone beyond the mark. Berowne rubs in his own moral: those absorbed in abstract studies overlook the practical affairs of life.

as towns with fire i.e. like the capture of towns set on fire during the attack: nothing is won.

of force Necessarily.

lie here Stay with us.

on mere necessity Simply out of hospitality to visitors.

affects Desires.

by might mast'red Overcome by sheer strength (of willpower). cf. 'might masters right'.

special grace i.e. dispensation (the setting aside of a law) by the King.

the laws at large i.e. the rest of the academy's conditions.

in attainder of Condemned to.

Suggestions Temptations.

loath Unwilling (to sign).

the last that will last keep his oath The one who will keep his oath longest. The repetition of 'last' is tautology.

quick recreation Lively amusement (to relieve the severity of the life of study).

haunted With Frequented by.

refined Cultured, polished.

planted Well established.

a mint of phrases i.e. a factory for coining expressions.

complements Accomplishments.

their mutiny Their quarrel (as opposites).

This child of fancy This man of imagination.

that Armado hight Who is called Armado. An archaic formality in narrative verse.

For interim As an interlude (relief).

tawny From the dark skin of its inhabitants.

lost in the world's debate Perished fighting. The name Armado may have been suggested by the Spanish Armada recently defeated (cf. the

King's epithet 'magnificent' applied to him below).

How you delight What pleasure you may take (in such a recital).

for my minstrelsy As if he were a minstrel of mine.

wight Man. Another poetic archaism.

fire-new Freshly minted (cf. 'mint' above). We now use 'brand-new' where 'brand' is the furnace.

knight Champion.

swain Rustic.

but short i.e. made less tedious by such amusement.

the duke's own person An English constable would be more familiar with 'his Grace' at the great house than a remote sovereign. As Armado speaks of Navarre also in the next scene as 'the duke', he cannot be as intimate with the King as he claims to be in V, 1,87.

This, fellow Indicating the King.

reprehend Malapropism for 'represent'.

tharborough Thirdborough, a junior constable.

contempts A curiously apt mistake for 'contents'.

How low . . . high words However base or trivial the matter, I expect it will be loftily expressed.

A high hope for a low heaven i.e. the heaven (suggested by 'I hope in God') is too worldly for a hope placed so high.

To hear, or forbear hearing (Patience) to endure listening to him or to stay away from the amusement he provides. An emendation of the Folio 'hearing' to 'laughing' is supported by Longaville's 'laugh moderately' in the next line.

to climb in the merriness To increase our mirth. Pun on climbing over a 'stile'.

The matter The substance (of the letter).

taken with the manner The pun comes from a misspelling of 'taken with the mainour', a legal phrase for caught red-handed.

In manner and form following A conventional phrase from the law-court, which Costard takes as three separate items. In his lame conclusion he leaves out the third, the 'following', as Berowne points out.

correction Punishment.

welkin's vicegerent Heaven's deputy on earth. An obsolete word not to be confused with 'vice-regent', the later 'viceroy'.

dominator An affected word (and rare) for 'ruler'.

fost'ring patron The function of a patron was to foster the chances of the artist he patronized, but this and much of what follows is the emptiest of verbiage.

'So it is—' A cliché, like the modern 'It so happens'.

in telling true To tell the truth (in Costard's opinion).

but so i.e. he is not worth much if he says he is speaking the truth.

other men's secrets Meaning his own.

besieged with sable-coloured melancholy Feeling sad. 'Sable' is a heraldic term for black, from the once prized fur of this animal.

Melancholy was one of the four 'humours' of the body which were believed to affect personal dispositions.

black-oppressing Repeating in other words 'sable' and 'besieged'.

thy health-giving air i.e. the atmosphere of your park.

as I am a gentleman A profession frequently found in Shakespeare.

The time When? The traditional catechizing method.

ycleped Another poetical archaism, for 'called', 'named'.

preposterous Contrary to regulation.

snow-white pen Formed from a goose's quill.

ebon-coloured Black as ebony.

north-north-east and by east Points of the compass were important in designing gardens.

curious-knotted With the skilfully made pattern of flower-beds known as 'knots'.

minnow An insignificant little fish. Johnson suggested 'minion'.

of thy mirth i.e. fit to be laughed at.

vassal Subordinate. Perhaps punning with 'vessel'.

sorted An obsolete dialectal form of 'consorted'.

continent canon Law forbidding relationship with women.

passion Grieve.

pricks Spurs.

meed of punishment A curiously contradictory expression.

a vessel of thy law's fury i.e. the recipient of the penalty.

at the least . . . notice At the slightest indication from you.

the best for the worst i.e. the most high-flown style for the commonest of offences.

so varied too Given that variety of category as well.

serve your turn i.e. the use of the term 'maid' will not save you.

serve my turn Suit me (as her lover).

pray a month Suggested by 'fast and pray'.

porridge Formerly stewed meat and vegetables, now oatmeal.

lay my head. . . hat i.e. bet my head against a much smaller stake, the hat that covers another's.

idle scorn Useless mockery.

true girl Honest girl.

prosperity Malapropism for 'adversity'. Similarly, 'affliction' for 'good fortune'.

sit thee down i.e. bear it patiently.

Act I Scene 2

Meanwhile, Armado, during a good deal of cross talk with his impertinent page, Moth, confesses to a melancholy mood caused by (1) the thought of three years' close study and (2) a sense of guilt for being in love with Jaquenetta. The constable enters with the dairy-maid and Costard. Armado makes an assignment with the former and despatches the latter to some lock-up in the care of Moth. The scene closes with a soliloquy in which Armado seeks consolation in examples of great men seduced by love for women.

Commentary

The writer of the 'euphuistic' letter is seen to be as fantastic in person as any foreigner, especially a Spaniard, could be expected to appear on an Elizabethan stage. His wit, however, is sorely worsted in word battles with two pert characters of inferior status. These exchanges prepare us for similar displays by the courtiers. Armado's melancholy, due as he thinks to guilt over a base passion, contrasts with the superficial gaiety and airy sentiment of the youthful pairs. The swiftness with which his rapier succumbs to Cupid's darts is matched by the equally swift and simultaneous conquest of no less than four young men recently committed on oath *not* to fall in love.

imp Mischievous child.
O Lord, sir Colloquial for 'indeed'.
part Distinguish between.
juvenal Youth. Obsolete form of 'juvenile'.
Signor This form of address (strictly *Señor* in Spanish) is derived from Latin *senior*, older person – hence the retort.
congruent epitheton Suitable epithet (original Greek form).
nominate Denominate, describe as.
appertinent Pertinent, suitable.
your old time Your age.
condign Well-deserved. Now used of punishment.
with the same praise i.e. apt because the eel is quick. Armado used 'quick' in the sense of the word in I,1,160, 'lively'.
heat'st my blood Angerest me.
I am answered I stand rebuked.
the mere contrary: crosses . . . him The very opposite. Moth hints that his master loves to feel coins (stamped with crosses) on his palm, but money does not often come his way.
ill at reck'ning Poor at arithmetic.
the spirit of a tapster The mentality of a barman (reckoning up the cost of drinks).
gamester Gambler.
varnish Polish (of refinement).
deuce-ace Two and one in dice.

base vulgar Common crowd. Tautology also in 'gross sum', above.

three studied i.e. the word 'three' looked at with the eyes.

dancing horse Possibly 'Morocco', a long famous horse, trained to perform tricks.

fine figure i.e. apt figure of speech, in the form of a comparison.

a cipher A nought (suggested by 'figure').

humour of affection Disposition of love.

reprobate Wicked.

ransom him . . . for Sell Desire (i.e. his infatuation) in exchange for.

new devised curtsy Newly invented manner of bowing.

outswear Cupid Forswear love.

More authority More examples to quote.

carriage Physical bearing. Gives rise to a pun in the next line.

carried the town-gates See Judges 16,3.

complexion Originally a combination (cf. 'complex') of the four 'humours' in different amounts, thus forming one individual disposition. In Shakespeare's day the colour and texture of the skin (especially of the face) were also an external indication of the character within.

all the four The chief 'humours' (liquids) of the body were once believed to be blood, phlegm, yellow bile and black bile; where one was predominant the character was respectively sanguine, phlegmatic, choleric or melancholy. We still speak of good and bad humour.'Humour' gradually became associated with fun.

Green Not one of the 'complexions', but traditionally the colour of youth, immaturity and hopefulness. cf. 'green geese' I,1,97.

a love of that colour Delilah was not Samson's first wife. Armado assumes he would have been attracted by her intellect!

a green wit This could mean either immature or well-preserved. Samson was bound by 'green withs'.

immaculate white and red i.e. perfect in her complexion.

maculate Spotted. ('Immaculate' means 'spotless'.) Wicked thoughts are often concealed behind innocent expressions.

Define Explain.

assist me He calls on his parents (with their characteristic qualities) to help him in composition.

invocation i.e. Moth's calling on his parents. The word is used of an appeal (to some god) for aid in the opening lines of a poem.

pathetical Full of feeling.

native From birth.

owe Possess.

against the reason of white and red Against judging by the proportion of these colours in the complexion.

ballet Ballad.

the King and the Beggar This story of King Cophetua was used in Percy's *Reliques* (Ballads) and by Tennyson in a short poem called 'The

Beggar Maid'. Armado adopted the comparison in his letter in IV,1,97.

very guilty of i.e. wrong in producing.

it would neither serve . . . tune Neither words nor air would be accepted today.

newly writ o'er Reworded.

example my digression Illustrate my straying from the right path. 'Transgression' has replaced this word.

precedent Earlier example, affording justification.

rational hind Sensible rustic. Or is Armado speaking in scorn of him as differing from the animals only in possessing reasoning powers? Costard is a mixture of sense and nonsense.

and yet 'Deserves' is understood.

light Loose-living. Word play on 'light', opposite of 'heavy'.

Forbear . . . past Wait until these people have gone.

penance The constable's mistake for 'pleasance' (Elizabethan for 'pleasure').

allowed for the day-woman Taken on the staff as the servant in the 'day' or dairy.

With that face? What a hope!

Fair weather after you! A few examples are to be found of this obsolete form of farewell. The fine weather is to accompany the traveller!

on a full stomach Pun on the stomach as the seat (then) of courage and as the organ which suffers most from a fast.

more bound to you Pun on (1) his being kept prisoner by Armado and (2) their dependence on him for their (poor) wages.

fellows Servants.

I will fast, being loose i.e. I will abstain from food willingly provided I am free. This leads to Moth's use of 'fast and loose' for 'cheating', from a game played by gipsies with a stick and a piece of string.

desolation Malapropism for 'consolation', or happiness. Cf. his similar phrase, 'the sour cup of prosperity', I,1,304.

some shall see A solemn pronouncement which proves empty of meaning.

too silent in their words This can only be a pun on 'words' and 'wards' or prison cells. He means 'less than silent', i.e. outspoken. This malapropism is followed by another: 'as little patience'.

affect Love.

base The three degrees of baseness indicated by Armado show the nature of his 'affection' for the 'base wench' of 54: the ground (neutral), her shoe (part of her apparel), her foot (part of her body).

argument of falsehood Proof of dishonesty.

familiar Attendant spirit.

butt-shaft Arrow without barbs, used in practice-shooting at the butts. Cupid's love darts are more powerful than any weapon.

too much odds Having too great an advantage.

a Spaniard's rapier i.e. his own weapon. Cf. l.70, where he compared it with Samson's strength.

first and second cause Probably from some vanished rules of duelling.

passado A forward thrust.

duello The laws of the duel (to which the word was later shortened).

disgrace Misfortune. cf. I,1,3, as if the term 'boy' were lacking in
  respect for a powerful god.

your manager He who has handled you.

extemporal god of rhyme Inspirer of extempore verse.

turn sonnet Compose verse.

Devise Compose (the words).

folio i.e. the largest size of page.

Revision questions on Act I

1 List all the clauses in the vow.

2 Contrast the attitudes to love of Berowne and Armado.

3 Write character sketches of (a) Costard, and (b) Moth, as they
appear in this Act.

Act II Scene 1

The Princess of France, having arrived in Navarre attended by
three ladies, sends her attendant lord, Boyet, to enquire if, like
other ladies, they are forbidden to enter the house, and to
inform the King that her business is urgent. Meanwhile she is
given character sketches of the three courtiers who have shared
in the royal vow. On his return Boyet has scarcely time to
explain that the ladies are to be accommodated away from the
house in pavilions, when the King and his companions appear.
He apologizes, and is presented with the French King's message.
Of 200,000 crowns spent by Navarre in the French King's wars,
half has, it is claimed, been repaid (though Navarre knows
nothing of it). The other half, the French King is unwilling to
refund and prefers to surrender the title to Aquitaine, which
stood surety; instead, he presses for a fresh loan of the first half.
In spite of this unreasonable request, Navarre gallantly offers to
pay it back if Boyet can produce proof of the French repayment.
After he leaves, the gentlemen return in succession to learn
more about their respective ladies. The final comment lies with
Boyet, who gives an extravagant account of the King's obvious
infatuation with the Princess.

Commentary

There is further artificiality in that each of the three courtiers has met or been seen previously by his respective lady, on individual visits to France. Each is reported on favourably by the very lady in whom he is, later in the scene, keenly interested. The symmetry is overpowering! The ladies' attitudes, however, change after finding that one clause in the vow, the veto on their entry to the palace, is being adhered to; the assumed antagonism is highlighted by the two preliminary skirmishes between Berowne and Rosaline (the first serving to give time for the King to read the document). A relationship of the Benedick and Beatrice kind (in *Much Ado about Nothing*) seems already to have been established. It gives prominence to this couple, further indicated by the less aggressive manner in which the other two infatuated courtiers cautiously seek second-hand information about their ladies from Boyet, presumably in full view of them. This same attendant French lord's superior tone in describing a minor kinglet head-over-ears in love is repaid by the contempt shown him in the last act in two of Berowne's speeches, one in Boyet's absence and the other soon after, in which he hears himself pilloried as a 'carry-tale' and a 'clown'.

dearest spirits Wits at their best.
what's his embassy Who is his ambassador.
parley Negotiate.
inheritor Owner (through inheritance).
perfections Highest accomplishments.
owe Possess.
plea i.e. the subject of negotiation.
Aquitaine, a dowry for a queen An educated Elizabethan would know
   that in the twelfth century Eleanor of Aquitaine brought so much
   territory to the English King, Henry II, that he held more land than
   the French King himself. During its occupation by the English and its
   eventual recovery it was split up into smaller provinces.
prodigal Unstinting, generous. The comparison with Nature is readily
   understood, though paradoxically expressed: Nature was hardly
   'prodigal' in making personal charms scarce, or in lavishing them all
   on one person. This highly artificial piece of flattery is suitably
   rebuked.
flourish Superfluous decoration, like the extra strokes added to a
   signature; 'painted', while inappropriate to 'flourish', adds the
   suggestion of an overdone painting.
utt'red Sold (put 'out' for sale).

sale Here the method of selling, i.e. exaggerated praise of the dealers themselves. The sentence means that beauty is more accurately assessed by the purchaser than by the vendor. The analogy from trade is continued by 'tell', 'counted', 'spending'.

I am less proud i.e. my modesty is greater than your conceit.

to task the tasker To set a (difficult) task to the taskmaster: confront him who has prohibited women from his Court with a visiting princess. Or it may be a retort to Boyet himself for indicating to the Princess her duty.

ignorant Unaware that.

all-telling fame Wide-spreading rumour.

his silent court Prolepsis, a figure of speech in which an effect is anticipated before it happens: the Court being approached would be silent later, because of the forbidden conversation with the ladies after their arrival, or because they would not be admitted.

to's seemeth It seems to us.

Bold of your worthiness Made bold by relying on your (ambassadorial) qualities.

best-moving Most eloquent.

fair solicitor Well-spoken advocate (*not* a lawyer).

craving quick dispatch Requiring to be dealt with immediately.

All pride is willing pride i.e. pride (unlike humility) needs no forcing on anyone; it is voluntary.

votaries Those who have sworn a vow.

beauteous heir Until the seventeenth century, 'heir' was used of both sexes.

Nothing becomes him ill . . . well i.e. he does gracefully whatever he is interested in doing.

soil of Defect in.

If virtue's gloss . . . soil Admitting the unsuitability of the word 'soil' (which suggests the tarnishing of a bright surface) to emphasize a defect.

matched with too blunt a will The words 'sharp' and 'blunt' seem balanced as opposites: a keen mind and slackness of resolution. 'Matched', however, means not only opposed to, but paired with: Longaville's intellect goes with an abrupt, insensitive manner, hence the cutting edge and the sparing of nobody (cf. his vicious penalty in I,1,122).

whose will still wills Whose resolve is constantly determined.

merry mocking lord A lord whose amusement is mocking others (like Jaques in *As You Like It*); a facetious cynic.

his humours His moods.

wither as they grow Shrivel up as their biting wit develops, like all precocious growths.

Of all that virtue love for virtue loved Loved for his virtue by all who love virtue.

Most power . . . ill With the greatest capacity to do harm and at the same time the least evil intention.

wit to make . . . good Ability to give evil an appearance of respectability.

shape to win grace . . . wit A physical appearance handsome enough to obtain favours without the need to possess any mental ability.

the Duke Alençon's i.e. her father's, according to 1.194. This prominent French noble was once a suitor for Queen Elizabeth's hand!

much too little . . . worthiness My account of his goodness as I saw it is grossly inadequate.

Was there with him i.e. at the Duke of Alençon's.

but a merrier man . . . withal I never spoke with a more humorous man, limiting humour to what is socially acceptable.

His eye begets . . . wit He finds an opportunity in everything he sees for making a witty remark.

the one doth catch She is now thinking in terms of two eyes.

conceit's expositor The utterer of the words that communicate the witty idea.

aged ears play truant i.e. adults leave what they are doing in order to listen (Synecdoche).

bedecking ornaments Decorations that decorate. Tautology, a figure of speech that is often effective in a language with two main sources for its vocabulary: Anglo-Saxon and Latin. Milton wrote in *Samson Agonistes* of the approaching Delilah: 'So bedecked, ornate, and gay'.

your fair approach Your distinguished arrival.

competitors Associates.

addressed Prepared.

He rather means i.e. he means rather (than seek a dispensation).

a dispensation A licence (to break his oath).

enter his unpeopled house 'Unpeopled' because they will not be able to enter it. Prolepsis, like 'silent court' in 1.24. The missing 'people' have been interpreted as servants to attend on the visitors.

I give you back again Not returning the complement (e.g. 'fair prince'), but declining the attribute 'fair', as she has not been given the treatment appropriate to it.

The roof of this court i.e. the sky (which belongs to God). A metaphor taken from the house in which she should have been received and not the park.

welcome . . . mine i.e. the welcome I have been given in the park is too degrading for a princess.

You shall be welcome Emphasis on the future. Is this a hint of some later reception in proper style after the vow has somehow been superseded?

I will be welcome Changing from the future simple to the future of determination, a distinction peculiar to English grammar.

Hear me, dear lady Begging to be excused.

He'll be forsworn Suggesting that some men's oaths are taken only to be broken, or else that he will be unable to resist her.

by my will A form of oath, this also conveys the idea of his using his willpower. Or 'not by my will' means 'not willingly'.

will shall break it The 'will' she used in 'I will be welcome'.

Where my lord so . . . ignorance i.e. if you knew nothing of this oath (and so had not sworn it) that would be wise, whereas the knowledge of it only shows your ignorance (of life).

sworn out house-keeping Taken an oath not to entertain.

deadly sin to keep that oath i.e. an offence against traditional hospitality. There are frequent allusions in contemporary literature to the dying practice of keeping open house.

sin to break it Because it has been sworn.

too sudden-bold Too blunt so soon after an introduction.

ill beseemeth me Is unbecoming to one of my rank.

Vouchsafe Deign, condescend. She hands him the document ('plea') referred to in l.7.

suddenly resolve me in my suit Give me a quick answer to the request I bring.

if suddenly I may If I *can* do it quickly

You will the sooner . . . away You will make the decision all the quicker in order to get me to leave.

Did I not dance . . . once? The beginning of the contest of wits between these two, which anticipates the similar but better developed skirmish between Benedick and Beatrice in *Much Ado About Nothing*. Brabant was a province of the Netherlands on the opposite frontier of France to Navarre.

quick Swift in repartee.

long of you that spur me Because of you who force me to go faster.

leave the rider in the mire Toss him who spurs it into the mud.

What time o'day A change of subject?

The hour that fools should ask A time of day which is obvious to all but fools, or the time (any time) when silly questions are asked.

fair befall your mask i.e. good luck to whoever is behind it. This suggests that Shakespeare originally intended the ladies to mask themselves on the approach of the King and the courtiers, but used the idea instead in V,2, omitting to remove this reference from the manuscript copy. As a brief interlude this passage was far too short for developing mistaken identities. And a word was needed to rhyme with 'ask'!

intimate Mention.

say that Assuming.

in surety of the which As a pledge for repayment.

not valued to the money's worth Not equal in value to a hundred thousand crowns.

that one half which is unsatisfied i.e. the second sum (conceding the receipt of the repayment of the first).

he doth demand to have repaid i.e. he asks for the repayment (or fresh loan) of the first sum while still owing for the second.

not demands . . . Aquitaine i.e. does not seek to resume his title over Aquitaine by paying back the sum needed to redeem it.

depart withal Dispense with.

so gelded as it is i.e. with parts cut off what was once a huge province.

so far From reason's yielding So far beyond what a reasonable man would consent to.

A yielding 'gainst some reason Some concession against my better judgement.

In so unseeming In thus not appearing.

repay it back Tautology.

arrest Seize upon as security.

acquittances Receipts.

special officers Officers dealing with specific contracts or 'specialties' (l.164).

Where that and other specialties are bound In which this and other documents are enclosed.

liberal reason Generous reasonableness.

Make tender of . . . worthiness Offer to one of your rank.

within my gates Gates separated the typical English mansion and its immediate precincts from the tree-studded park outside.

so received . . . heart An extravagant excuse for offering a tent for a bedroom!

fair harbour Handsome accommodation.

consort Attend.

commend Praise. Or possibly mimicking the King by offering her suitable lodging in his heart (cf. l.173).

do my commendations i.e. sing my praises.

to see it And so verify that he has a heart when he has 'commended' her to it.

heard it groan i.e. his heart.

let it blood Bleed it (the 'fool').

My physic My medical knowledge.

prick't i.e. draw the blood.

No point Not at all. A Gallicism from the negative construction *ne* . . . *point*, with a pun on the point of a knife.

from long living i.e. from the torment of continued existence.

stay Stop. Both words have the same double meaning: (1) I cannot linger here thanking you, and (2) I cannot refrain from thanking you. The wit is cramped as much as sharpened by the demands of rhyme. Perhaps there is a hit at long graces before meals.

light in the light A loose woman when seen clearly. A strange pun, in keeping with his character, as already hinted at in l.50, spoken by the very lady thus referred to; but his attitude changes when he learns her identity (II,1,205).

She hath but one Meaning she cannot part with it, and playing on Longaville's expression 'I desire (you to tell me) her name'.

God's blessing on your beard! Ironical: 'Confound you for an elderly quibbler'. References to beards could be insulting.

heir Heiress. See note on l.41. Presumably this is a sister sharing the inheritance.

her name in the cap The name of the lady wearing a cap.

hap Fortune. A meaningless rhyming word.

To her will To her own inclination. 'Wedded' could mean 'pledged to marry' or, simply, 'attached, as to a habit'.

Farewell to me . . . you Berowne's hail-farewell manner is continued by Boyet with a piece of stage nonsense: 'You say farewell to me and I say you are welcome to go'.

but a jest But is a jest.

but a word Is expressed only in a word.

to take him at his word Referring to the play on 'farewell'.

to grapple A naval term for seizing hold of an enemy ship with a 'grapnel' in order to board her.

board Clamber on to the enemy's deck.

Two hot sheeps Two armed vessels. 'Sheep' and 'ship' were close enough in pronunciation to allow for numerous puns.

unless we feed on your lips He and Berowne are to be changed from warships to grazing sheep only in the sense of pasturing on her by kissing her. This would have been more appropriate to Rosaline, but the names of the ladies have been confused in the various texts. 'Sweet lamb' is a mere interjection.

no common, though several Not pasture for all comers, though a pair. A pun on common and private land, held 'severally' (individually). Her lips are 'several' in two senses: separate or divided, and private.

book-men i.e. devoted to three years of study.

abused Wasted.

By the heart's still rhetoric . . . eyes By the look in the eyes, which reveals the otherwise unexpressed feelings of the heart.

Deceive me not now The subject is 'observation'. The awkwardness of the construction is due to the rhyme.

infected Smitten with 'affection'.

behaviours Bodily movements.

we lovers Boyet has been suspected by some critics of jealousy of any pretender to the hand of his mistress.

make their retire To the court of his eye i.e. withdraw (for closer defence – and resultant confusion) to the fortified mansion within its courtyard. The metaphor is repeated in l.241: 'all his senses were lock'd in his eye'.

peeping through desire i.e. all his senses peeping out of his eyes through desire to behold her (as at a crowded window).

like an agate . . . impressed With your picture impressed on it (his heart), like the figure carved in miniature on an agate ring.

Proud with his form i.e. (his heart) proud of its shape (carrying your imprint).

in his eye pride expressed i.e. this pride being shown in the look in his eye.

impatient to speak and not see i.e. unable to suffer its limitation to uttering words.

in his eyesight to be This line and the next two suggest confusion among this garrison of the senses, as they crowd into the visual organ to have a look.

make their repair Make their way (to a place, here the eyeball).

To feel only looking on fairest of fair i.e. to enjoy the 'sight' of beauty only through feeling.

tend'ring their own worth . . . glassed Displaying their value by the name of the place where they were produced.

glassed Set in crystal.

point you Beckon to you.

margent The margin of a page in which explanatory notes could be written.

amazes Looks of amazement.

gazes Admiring stares.

for my sake i.e. to help me win my bet (that he and his are yours for the asking).

our pavilion The tent in the park.

disposed Contemporary abbreviation of 'disposed to jest'. Boyet is in a facetious mood.

But to speak (Disposed) only to say (what the look in Navarre's eye means).

made a mouth of his eye i.e. put into words what his looks express.

adding a tongue i.e. offering himself as a (true) interpreter.

love-monger Dealer in love as a commodity.

Venus The goddess of love was the mother of Cupid, which in Maria's invented mythology would make her daughter of the 'grim' Boyet.

Do you hear Listen to me (and stop your nonsense).

No Rosaline continues the play on the senses: she cannot hear her mistress's command, but she can see the way (to the pavilion).

too hard for me Uncontrollable.

Act III Scene 1

Armado sends his page to set Costard free, but not before an odd conversation in which Moth gives his master satiric advice on being in love, while laughing at him behind his back. When he returns with Costard we are treated to further word-play started by Moth's reference to the broken shin suffered by Costard when scrambling out of his prison.

Armado scents a riddle and calls for an 'envoy', mistaken by the simple Costard for ointment. He declares he prefers a natural remedy in the form of a plantain, which leads somehow to a goose. Armado then explains that he has freed him to take a letter to Jaquenetta, giving him the meanest of tips as a 'remuneration'. No sooner has he gone than Berowne arrives: having met Costard before and seeing in him an honest messenger and one least to be suspected, Berowne gives him *his* love letter, which he calls a 'legal document', at the same time rewarding him generously with a shilling as a 'guerdon'. Then, like Armado in I,2, he concludes the scene with a self-examining soliloquy, in which the contempt is shared between himself and the one who has ensnared him.

Commentary

The slightness of the plot and the excessive verbiage – from fine-spun conceits to homespun exchanges – with which the dialogue of the play is loaded, are well exemplified in this central act, which, like Act II, consists of a single scene. Its main concern is the despatch of two letters, written by two tormented admirers, surprised and almost humiliated to find themselves in love. Moth, the observant page, expatiates on the signs of love in his master; Berowne recognizes at some length the same signs in himself. Moth sees Armado's arms crossed on his 'thin-belly doublet'; Berowne addresses the boy-god Cupid as 'lord of folded arms'. Love is regarded here as an affliction, for which there may be a remedy; the literary forms, however, in which love is often expressed are no 'salve' or 'l'envoy' for an actual broken shin, physical injury that is apparently soon forgotten in comparing the monetary values of a 'guerdon' and a 'remuneration'. Moth's puns and Costard's blunders compete for the laughter of the audience.

make passionate . . . hearing Move me to passion through my ears, or, simply, sing me a love song.
Concolinel Perhaps from a contemporary French song, or the title of one.
tenderness of years Affected expression for 'young fellow'.
give enlargement to Set free.
festinately In haste.
a French brawl A dance, mistaken by Armado for the usual word.
canary to it Dance in a fantastic fashion (the name of this Spanish dance comes from the Canary Islands).
humour it Give expression to the mood of love.
penthouse-like o'er the shop Worn like the sloping roof projecting over an open shop – thus shading the eyes.

thin-belly doublet The doublet was a close-fitting jacket often padded for fashion's sake. This one suggests the wasting away of the lover.

the old painting i.e. a portrait with the hands hidden by the artist to save the trouble of their detailed painting.

a snip and away A snatch and off somewhere else (like his own effort in I,2).

betray Seduce.

nice A word that has had an infinitude of meanings. Here 'wanton', as made clear by the parenthesis.

make them men of note . . . these Make those who are given to such practice conspicuous in the public eye.

my penny of observation i.e. it cost me little but keeping my eyes open. cf. 'a pennyworth of wit'.

But O . . . The hobby-horse is forgot Perhaps a line from an old song. This was an imitation animal fastened to the waist of a dancer who pranced about in village fêtes. Armado is offended, since the word was also used for a prostitute.

hackney Hired horse.

By heart i.e. committed to memory.

out of heart Downcast.

A man, if I live i.e. grow to manhood.

this . . . instant i.e. (prove) this triple statement immediately. A pun on 'prove' meaning (1) turn out to be, and (2) demonstrate. The demonstration takes the form of word-twisting.

well sympathized With two features that harmonize: the horse (the carrier) is Costard, the ass is Armado.

Minime Not in the least (Latin).

too swift i.e. too quick to contradict. A play on 'slow'.

smoke of rhetoric i.e. discharge of logic.

Thump Stride with a heavy, dull sound. Used by Moth for the firing of a cannon.

acute juvenal Quick-witted youth.

in thy face i.e. looking up at the sky.

gives thee place Yields to you.

costard A type of large apple ('costermonger' is a derivative). It also meant a head, hence the 'wonder'.

l'envoy The concluding stanza or final couplet of a 'ballade' of which the main part was the 'moral'.

No egma Costard thinks that Armado's words are those of a would-be physician preparing to deal with a broken shin. He is afraid of these strange-sounding remedies and calls for a simple herbal remedy (a 'plain' one).

salve in the mail Healing ointment carried in a bag.

plantain A wild plant whose leaf is still used for treating bruises.

By virtue A meaningless exclamation.

thy silly thought, my spleen Your ignorant remark makes me laugh (the spleen was held to be the source of excessive mirth as well as ill-temper).

the inconsiderate This ignorant man (incapable of proper
consideration).

Is not l'envoy a salve? Here Moth is confusing (or pretending to confuse)
Costard's salve with *salve*, Latin greeting, coming at the beginning of a
letter or conversation, and sometimes at the end.

epilogue Strictly the concluding part of a speech, summing up or making
an appeal ('peroration' is the Latin form). Later it came to be used as a
final speech at the end of a play, sometimes addressed to the audience
(like Armado's in this play, short as it is).

obscure precedence Some previous statement that was not clear; 'that
hath tofore been sain' is therefore tautological.

I will example it This illustration of an envoy, as far as 'adding four',
does not appear in the first Folio.

stayed the odds Countered the odds (by adding four).

ending in the goose i.e. as spoken by Armado! Was this why Moth had
the rhyme repeated, changing rôles with his master?

sold him a bargain Made a fool of him.

your pennyworth The price of a goose?

To sell a bargain . . . loose i.e. making a fool of someone is as clever as
cheating.

a fat goose Costard's new conception of 'l'envoy'.

he ended the market From the proverbial three women and a goose that
made a market.

sensibly With feeling.

Thou hast no feeling in it i.e. *Your* shin was not broken.

more matter An increase of pus.

enfranchise Liberate, set free.

Frances Costard's misunderstanding of 'enfranchise'.

I smell some l'envoy, some goose i.e. there is promise of something tasty.

enfreedoming Restoring to freedom. A clumsy word, soon replaced by
'enlarging'.

immured Shut up within walls.

restrained Kept from moving about.

captivated Made captive (now fascinated).

bound It is a habit of Armado's to round off a list of learned words with
the simplest term.

my purgation The clearing me of the charge against me. Applied
wrongly by Costard to the person of Armado.

durance Imprisonment. Survives only in the phrase 'durance vile'.

significant Intimation.

ward of Guard over.

the sequel That which follows, especially the continuation of a story.
Another literary term like 'l'envoy'. 'Sequel' had another contemporary
meaning, 'follower'.

ounce of man's flesh i.e. the diminutive Moth.

incony Jew Costard, who has mistaken 'adieu' for 'a Jew' may be using
rhyming slang for 'money'.

look to his remuneration i.e. see what Armado has placed in Costard's hand, which proves to be three-farthings, a silver coin issued only in Elizabeth's reign.

inkle Piece of linen tape. He imagines himself making a purchase and bargaining his three-farthings against the penny asked for the tape.

it carries it i.e. the sound of such a word will clinch the bargain.

out of this word Without using the word 'remuneration' (to impress the salesman).

exceedingly well met Berowne has discovered a messenger whom he knows, though he expresses no surprise at finding him out of prison.

carnation Flesh-coloured.

sealed-up counsel Legal advice in a sealed envelope. A pretence to avoid suspicion of a love-letter (Costard knows what he was put in prison for).

guerdon Reward.

a 'leven-pence farthing better Berowne is more generous or has better means than Armado. His tip is a shilling.

in print Exactly as ordered.

Gardon Costard's vocabulary has been further enlarged.

beadle to a humorous sigh i.e. prompt to 'arrest' any sigh expressing the melancholy of love.

domineering pedant o'er the boy A schoolmaster tyrannizing over Cupid.

wimpled Blindfolded.

purblind Quite blind.

wayward Capricious. Falling in love is traditionally a matter of chance.

senior-junior, giant-dwarf i.e. balancing centuries-old worship with perennial youth, great powers with a baby figure.

Dan Don, a form of address.

Regent of Ruler over.

folded arms The sad posture of a pining lover.

Liege Lord. In five lines there are eight different words for a ruler over others.

plackets Slits or pockets in women's skirts.

codpieces Pockets, often ornamental, worn in front of the breeches.

trotting paritors Wandering 'apparitors', on the look-out for sexual offenders to summon before an ecclesiastical court.

a corporal of his field His adjutant.

tumbler's hoop Acrobat's hoop, decorated with coloured ribbons.

I sue? I pay court to a lady?

like a German clock i.e. an unreliable piece of mechanism (early models had their faults).

out of frame Out of order (cf. 'frame of mind').

being a watch A hit at the night watch ('never going right')?

being watched A change to the passive – to see that she does not go astray.

perjur'd i.e. having broken his contract not to love.

the worst of all The most flirtatious (Rosaline).

whitely Pale-faced, by contrast with her dark locks.

pitch balls Pitch when heated has a liquid glint.

do the deed Make love.

Argus The possessor of a hundred eyes, placed by Juno to watch Io, one of her priestesses, with whom Jupiter (her husband) was in love.

eunuch Strictly, the guardian of a harem.

a plague i.e. a punishment.

almighty, dreadful, little The same paradox as in l.175.

groan The last word in this sequence implies rejection.

some Joan This once aristocratic name had, in Shakespeare's day, lost social standing and was almost synonymous with kitchen-maids (cf. the 'greasy Joan' of the winter song at the end).

Revision questions on Acts II and III

1 How are the three courtiers described by their respective ladies?

2 Which happenings are most unlikely in these two Acts? Does their improbability matter?

3 One character appears in both Acts. Contrast his two appearances.

Act IV Scene 1

The Princess and her attendants have risen early, as a forester is with them for the deer hunting. After quibbling with him over the meaning of 'the fairest shoot', as applied to a woman, she professes pity for the animal she must hit to qualify for such a title.

Costard arrives and, having clumsily identified the 'head lady', hands her Armado's letter instead of Berowne's. Though Boyet points out that the letter is addressed to one Jaquenetta, the Princess mischievously tells him to read it out aloud. He identifies the author by the signature, but Costard insists that it comes from Berowne. The princess hands it to Rosaline and leaves her to be teased by Boyet for having a suitor. Finally, Costard is left to *his* clownish but mercifully brief soliloquy.

Commentary

There is no hint whether Costard exchanged the two letters accidentally or intentionally; either would be in character. In this scene Armado's letter reaches a wrong destination; Berowne's does so in the next scene (with an entirely new set of characters to offset the similarity in the action). Costard is present at the reading aloud of both extravagant effusions: any satisfaction he may derive from the mistake is not evident. While the Princess hands Armado's missive to Rosaline to put away, Holofernes in the next scene despatches that of Berowne to the King, thus preparing the most dramatic of the play's surprises.

The Princess's sensitive opening remarks on killing to gain a title are followed after her departure by ribald punning, such as that on 'suitor' and 'shooter', and play on the two kinds of 'horned' victim; in Costard's closing soliloquy (in rhymed couplets of no known metre) we are left in some doubt about who is being triumphed over, Armado or Boyet?

steep-up rising Sharp gradient.
mounting mind Ambitious personality. A pun on the King's 'mount', or his mounting the hill.
our despatch i.e. the answer to the message we brought, which will despatch us back again.
play the murderer in i.e. take a shot at a deer with a cross-bow.
stand A constructed 'hide'.
the fairest shoot The best shot.
I am fair I am light of hair.
thereupon thou speak'st the fairest shoot i.e. you speak of me as the fairest shot because of the colour of my hair.
say no i.e. deny my fairness (of shot) by saying 'I meant not so'.
short-lived pride i.e. her pleasure in the compliment was quickly destroyed by his denial that she was 'fair'.
Yes, madam, fair i.e. Yes, I meant 'fair' (seeking safety in the ambiguity of the single word).
never paint me now i.e. after this argument don't flatter me with insincere compliments.
Where fair is not Where there is no beauty.
mend the brow Improve the features ('brow' to rhyme with 'now').
good my glass My dear mirror. 'Good my friend' usually introduced a protest.
foul words Uncomplimentary remarks. 'Foul' is the opposite of 'fair'.
more than due More than is their due.
inherit Possess. The country-bred forester has proved a true courtier.

saved by merit Confirmed by my deserving to be called 'fair' (her accurate shooting?).

O heresy in fair The doctrine that saving grace from God was not bestowed, but earned by merit, was a 'heresy' then gaining ground.

fit for these days i.e. when heretics abound.

A giving hand . . . praise i.e. those who give, however base their character, are to be praised for it.

mercy goes to kill Pity (for dumb animals) is prepared to kill against its better instincts.

shooting well is then accounted ill i.e. to score a hit seems a crime.

save my credit in the shoot Shoot well enough to be accredited a 'fair shoot'.

Not wounding If I don't hit a deer (my reason will be that I was prevented by pity).

If wounding If I would without killing (my reason will be that I was showing off my marksmanship, doing it only to be praised, and not as a hunter). Some editors interpret 'mercy' as killing outright, in preference to merely wounding, but the following argument takes the line here suggested.

out of question Undoubtedly.

Glory grows guilty . . . crimes i.e. those who have achieved fame by cruel deeds often are later full of remorse.

an outward part i.e. something which should have nothing to do with inner feelings.

We bend . . . heart i.e. we force our natural feelings in that direction (of killing).

the poor deer's blood . . . ill The blood of the poor deer which I have no desire to harm.

curst Shrewish. A word used frequently of Katharine in *The Taming of the Shrew*.

self-sovereignty Rule over oneself, autonomy (carried a stage further when the wife tries to subdue her husband, as in the next line).

the commonwealth This ideal community of abstainers from women's company.

dig-you-den Rustic for 'give you a good evening', or else a mis-print.

the head lady Costard is as much astray with titles as with technical terms.

The thickest and the tallest The Princess gives a literal interpretation to 'greatest' and 'highest'.

as slender as my wit As narrow as my understanding.

maids' girdles The waist-belts of these young ladies (whom he takes to be very junior to the 'head lady').

the thickest here The waists of boy actors taking the ladies' parts would not be uniformly slender!

What's your will, sir? Bridling at something far more insulting than the forester's 'foul words'.

O thy letter! Give me the letter (as I know him). Rosaline is strangely silent throughout this incident.

capon (1) a fat chicken (2) a love-letter (cf. the French use of *poulet*). 'Carve' refers to the chicken, 'break up' to the letter.

I am bound to serve It is my duty to wait upon you.

mistook Misdirected or wrongly delivered.

importeth Concerns (has importance for).

the neck (1) the narrow part of the seal; (2) the capon's neck.

heroical vassal Bold servitor.

illustrate Illustrious.

King Cophetua This legendary ruler of an African kingdom despised women until he fell in love with Penelophon, a beggar-maid.

pernicious and indubitate Wicked and undoubted.

Zenelophon Penelephon; this misprint occurs in Folios and Quartos.

veni, vidi, vici (I came, I saw, I conquered): the much-quoted brevity with which Julius Caesar reported his swift defeat of Pharnaces, King of Pontus.

annothanize Annotate (coined by Armado).

videlicet Namely (Latin).

catastrophe Strictly the catastrophe is the change of fortune leading to the end of a drama; later it acquired the bad sense of a disaster. Here Armado uses it for the conclusion, a triumphant one. It sounds to a later audience like a malapropism, but such a tissue of nonsense does not bear close examination.

exchange Get by exchange.

tittles Trifles. The 'titles' could be rights to property. 'Tittles' could also be small strokes of the pen compared with whole headings, the 'titles'.

profane Defile (by treating what is sacred as a common object). The normal lover would speak of 'profaning' the foot of the beloved, but Armado never forgets the lowly status of Jaquenetta.

dearest design of industry The best possible effort of my pen. Permutations of the various meanings of 'design' and 'industry' can produce a host of unsatisfactory renderings.

Nemean lion Local Greek monster killed by Hercules with his bare hands.

Submissive fall i.e. the lion lies down with the lamb.

from forage Instead of hunting.

repasture Food (to carry away for devouring in his 'den' which rhymes with 'then'). These last six lines follow the ryhme scheme of the sextet, or second part of a sonnet. This compound from 'repast' and 'pasture' is the only recorded instance of something so incompatible with a carnivorous animal!

indited Composed.

vane Weathercock. Pun on feathers and vanity?

better i.e. a better example of verbiage.

I am much deceived . . . style If I am not mistaken, the style is familiar.

Else your memory . . . erewhile You would have a bad memory if you ever forgot your first reading of a passage in a style like this.

phantasime Fantastical person.

Monarcho The title assumed by a mad Italian who haunted Elizabeth's court and thought himself the ruler of the world.
book-mates Fellow-students.
mistaken Taken to the wrong address.
put up this Put it away. (Why?)
thine Your turn.
continent Container, i.e. the sum of all beauty.
she that bears the bow i.e. the 'shooter', a pun on 'suitor' (same pronunciation, almost).
Finely put off! Well parried (praising herself).
kill horns Shoot deer.
if horns . . . miscarry If horns fail to be applied to a certain husband whose wife will be unfaithful to him within a year.
If we choose by the horns If it is a matter of husbands who deserve to be betrayed.
Finely put on Struck home (praising himself).
wrangle Engage in a battle of wits.
at the brow i.e. where the deer carries his horns.
come upon thee Attack you.
a man when . . . boy i.e. very old (Pepin died in 768).
Queen Guinever The wife of King Arthur.
Thou canst not hit it Popular dance song.
A mark marvellous well shot A target well hit.
O, mark but that mark! Just observe that target.
prick A mark pricked in the centre of the target.
mete Aim.
Wide o' the bow hand Missed on the left side.
your hand is out i.e. not on form.
clout The central mark, a pin painted white.
upshoot Best shot.
cleaving the pin Hitting the centre.
greasily Coarsely, indecently.
at pricks In shooting arrows.
rubbing Of one bowl against another.
owl Wiseacre.
swain Rustic. Ironic, coming from Costard.
O' my troth In faith.
incony Delightful (conscious irony?).
handful of wit Minute joker.
pathetical nit Pitiable insect (another rhyming word); sounds quite modern!
Sola! A hunting cry.

Act IV Scene 2

Holofernes the Pedant, Nathaniel the Parson, and Dull the Constable have been discussing the deer shot by the Princess, when they are approached by Jaquenetta, accompanied by her admirer Costard, who has given her the other letter, addressed by Berowne to Rosaline, telling her that it is from Armado. Called upon to read it, Nathaniel does so, in a tone unsuited to the sonneteer's passionate declaration of his abandonment of his vow to study in order to sing (imperfectly) the praises of his lady.

The discrepancy between this eulogy in verse and the coarse character of the woman who has received it strikes Holofernes; consulting the address on the packet, he realizes a mistake has been made and bids Jaquenetta take the letter straight to the King, a second mistake which creates trouble for its author in the next scene. The pedant clears the stage for it by inviting both the parson and the constable to join him as fellow-guests at the house of the father of one of his pupils.

Commentary

Acts IV and V are regarded by some as an improvement on what has gone before: perhaps, finding the Spanish Knight wearing a bit thin, they welcome new figures of fun in characters – not from abroad, but from the nearest English village, one adjoining the park of the King of Navarre! Here are parson, schoolmaster and constable. While the two bookmen air their learning, Nathaniel playing second fiddle to the overpowering pedagogue, the constable keeps discreetly within the limits of his rustic intelligence. The deer (unwillingly struck with an arrow from the Princess's bow) is no 'old grey doe' but a 'pricket'; to prove his authority on such matters Dull propounds the riddle of the four-week-old moon. But he is shrewd enough, however, to recognize the ingratiating flattery in the curate's remarks – not that Holofernes is backward in self-praise or in reciting his atrocious verse. In Scene 1 a cultured audience gave short shrift to Armado's fantastic epistle; here Berowne's quite Shakespearian sonnet is contemptuously dismissed as much inferior to Ovid.

reverend The modern word might be 'respectable'.
in the testimony of a good conscience i.e. as any honest man would confirm.
sanguis Blood (Latin).
in blood In perfect condition.
pomewater A large, juicy apple (obsolete).

in the ear of *Coelo*, the sky i.e. on a lofty branch of the tree.

crab Crab-apple.

the epithets are sweetly varied i.e. a nice selection of definitions (not the descriptive kind of epithets).

a buck of the first head A male fallow deer in its fifth year.

Sir Nathaniel· The address for a curate who had not a Master's degree.

haud credo I don't believe it (Latin emphatic negative). In the ears of Dull, 'old grey doe'.

a pricket A buck in its second year.

intimation Suggestion. Followed by a string of meaningless abstractions: 'insinuation', a stealthy hint; 'explication', explanation; 'replication', repetition.

facere To make (Latin).

undressed Untrimmed. Followed by another string, this time of synonyms from various activities, ending in 'unconfirmed', unauthorized.

ratherest By this affectation Holofernes probably means 'preferably' or 'even more so'.

insert Substitute.

Twice sod Twice boiled. From the archaic verb 'seethe', past participle 'sod', of which 'sodden', very wet, survives. From *bis coctus* (Latin for twice cooked) we have 'biscuit'.

only sensible in the duller parts Capable of feeling only in the non-intellectual parts of his body.

barren plants i.e. dull specimens.

we thankful . . . more than he i.e. we who have cultivated tastes and emotions should be grateful for those faculties in us which bear more fruit.

were there a patch set on learning i.e. if one could find a fool anxious to learn.

omne bene All is well (Latin).

being of an old father's mind With the wisdom of one of the ancients.

brook Endure.

book-men Scholars.

Cain's birth Birth of Adam's eldest son.

Dictynna One of the several names of Diana, twin sister of Apollo and goddess of hunting, chastity and the moon (Luna or Phoebe).

raught Reached. An earlier form, cf. 'teach–taught'.

allusion Reference to something without naming it (here the moon).

in the exchange i.e. with Adam instead of Cain.

collusion Mistake for 'allusion'.

God comfort thy capacity Heaven help your mental capacity.

pollusion A non-word.

extemporal Extemporary (obsolete).

Perge Proceed (Latin).

so it shall please you to On condition that you.

abrogate Usually 'repeal'; here, 'do without'.

affect the letter Use alliteration (repetition of initial letters).

argues facility Proves my ready skill in composition.

preyful Killing much prey (rare).

sore A four-year-old, with obvious pun to follow.

yell Then used of hounds.

L to sore i.e. L prefixed as the Latin symbol for fifty.

sorel A three-year-old.

one more L i.e. two fifties.

If a talent be a claw . . . talent i.e. if a talent (familiar perhaps to Dull as the everyday pronunciation of a bird's 'talon') is a claw, see how Nathaniel claws (secondary meaning of 'flatters') Holofernes by praising his talents.

forms Terms of rhetoric.

revolutions Turnings over in the mind.

begot in the ventricule of memory Conceived in the part of the brain where the memory functions.

pia mater Membrane covering the brain (medical Latin term).

delivered Born.

upon the mellowing of occasion i.e. when the time is ripe.

commonwealth Community at large.

Mehercle! Exclamation, 'By Hercules!'

want no instruction Not lack for teaching.

vir sapit qui pauca loquitur That man is wise who speaks few words (Latin).

quasi person A textual riddle. The Latin *quasi* (as if) could mean 'almost the same as'. The pedantic Holofernes puns on Jacquenetta's rustic pronunciation of 'person' (pierce-'un) and the verb 'pierce' (root of the name Percy); the word 'parson', priest of a parish, is ultimately derived from 'persona', actor, from the mask 'spoken through' in classical times.

hogshead Barrel of wine (to be broached or 'pierced'); also a thickhead.

lustre of conceit in a turf of earth i.e. a bright piece of wit from a clod.

Fauste, precor . . . ruminat 'O Faustus, I beg of you, while the whole herd is chewing the cud in the cool shade'. A quotable line from Mantuan, fifteenth-century Italian poet, whose Latin works were sixteenth-century school books.

Chi non ti vede . . . pretia He who sees thee not, values thee not (Italian).

Ut, re . . . fa Notes of the musical scale. Schoolmasters taught singing.

Horace Latin poet 65–68 BC best known for his Odes, school texts for centuries.

and very learned Nathaniel has been glancing over the letter while the impatient Holofernes reels off his irrelevant scraps of learning.

staff Now 'stave' (formed from the plural of 'staff'). Used in musical scores.

Lege, domine Read, master (Latin).

swear to love Seal my love with an oath.

never faith . . . vowed i.e. only devotion to beauty can keep faith.

Those thoughts . . . bowed i.e. my firm adherence to what I have sworn melted away in your presence.

Study his bias leaves i.e. the student abandons his beloved books.

makes his book thine eyes Berowne had developed this idea in I,1,80.

the mark The goal in life.

Well learned is that tongue . . . commend i.e. he who can praise thee sufficiently is the true scholar.

which is to me some praise i.e. from which I can claim some credit.

admire Wonder at.

Thy eye . . . sweet fire i.e. your eyes and voice have god-like powers of lightning and thunder, but when not angered they shed light and music.

this wrong This presumption.

apostrophas The apostrophe indicating an omitted letter. The Latin form ended in *-us*. There are five in the sonnet, none of which affects the accent or the metre.

supervise the canzonet Glance over the song.

only numbers ratified Merely the metre observed (the correct number of syllables per line). By 'cadence' he may mean rhythm.

caret It is lacking (Latin).

Ovidius Naso Roman poet generally known as Ovid (43BC–AD17), whose works were well known to Shakespeare, mostly from translations.

'Naso' The ablative case of *nasus,* Latin for 'nose'.

smelling out Discovering (for later imitation).

odoriferous flowers Metaphor for rich poetical phrases.

jerks of invention Strokes of wit.

tired i.e. harnessed for a performance in which the animal closely follows its rider's movements.

from one Monsieur Berowne Author's slip? in ll.89–9, it was 'sent me from Don Armado'. One wonders exactly what Costard has been up to.

strange Foreign. Another slip: Berowne is not French. Did Jacquenetta get this false information from Costard who heard the Princess say of Berowne 'he's a good friend of mine' (IV,1,55)?

overglance The only recorded instance of this affected word.

superscript Anything (e.g. name and address) written above the main part of a communication. The opposite of 'subscript' (both words obsolete). Holofernes's false pedantry is also responsible for 'intellect' (written contents) and 'nomination' (name).

party Person. A legalistic variant, later vulgarized.

votaries Those who have taken a vow.

framed Composed.

sequent Follower.

by the way of progression On its journey.

Trip and go Familiar refrain in a dancing song.

concern much Be of great importance. Does he recognize a breach of his oath by one of the King's 'votaries'?

Stay not thy compliment Don't wait to pay your respects on leaving (your duty).

Have with thee Away with you.

a certain father A religious authority in the first Christian centuries.

colourable colours Plausible excuses?

Marvellous well for the pen i.e. I admired the penmanship.

on my privilege I have On the strength of my friendship.

ben venuto Welcome (Italian).

those verses i.e. Berowne's sonnet.

I beseech your society I request your company thither.

saith the text i.e. taken from a 'father'.

certes Certainly.

concludes it Sums it up.

pauca verba Few words (Latin), i.e. let us be going.

at their game i.e. hunting.

recreation Refreshment (the dinner).

Act IV Scene 3

This scene requires three individual hiding places – pillars or shrubs – though possibly such concealment is unnecessary, as each successive lover seems too absorbed in his thoughts and in the recitation of his particular composition to be sufficiently observant to notice he is being spied on.

Berowne is first on the scene, groaning over his predicament and wishing the others were also in love. Thereupon the King enters and has barely time to read his poem when Longaville declaims his sonnet. He in his turn hides when he sees Dumain. This time practically all the comment comes from Berowne, each exclamation of Dumain's receiving a mocking echo which only the theatre audience catches. Then, in the order 'last in, first out', Longaville steps forth to rebuke Dumain, is immediately rebuked in his turn by the King, who is allowed a lengthy dressing-down of the other two before himself being exposed by Berowne, who does not hesitate to include his sovereign in his sweeping condemnation (it was the King's idea, anyway).

This is the psychological moment for Costard and Jaquenetta to approach with a letter (treasonable, according to Holofernes) which the King loftily hands to Berowne to read. The latter, who has already tried to make a bolt for it, tears it up, but Dumain finds his signature on one of the pieces. Cursing Costard, Berowne confesses that the lovesick courtiers now number four and then proceeds to justify their oath-breaking as due to Nature; since all have erred, there is no one to judge. He defends the beauty of his dark-haired Rosaline against the fashionable idea that fair hair is the ideal colour.

Appealed to by the others to use his wit to find some excuse for their perjury, Berowne embarks once more on his doctrine that the highest studies find inspiration in a woman's eyes. The four gallants, thus encouraged, prepare to take the field under Cupid's banner and (more literally) lay on some entertainment.

Commentary

Four lovers successively caught out inditing love poems to the ladies to whom they have spontaneously succumbed (more embarrassing to them possibly than their perjured signatures) could well be criticized as too artificially symmetrical, but there is some variety to relieve it. All, with proper dramatic irony, wish, when alone with their sighs and tears, for the others to be equally involved – a wish that is almost immediately granted:

Berowne: if the other three were in.
King (seeing Longaville): In love, I hope:
Longaville: Am I the first . . .?
Dumain: would the king, Berowne, and Longaville,
        Were lovers, too!

Dumain produces an appropriate epigram: 'none offend where all alike do dote'. The scene is dominated by Berowne who counts them in, and by his comments seems secure of triumph.

The series of rebukes is also varied: Longaville reproaches Dumain for desiring others to share his perjury; the King upbraids the two of them in alternate lines, quoting from the 'guilty rhymes' he has listened to; Berowne seizes on the negative irony used by his sovereign on his companions when he reproduces Navarre's fantastic simile: 'Your eyes do make no coaches.'

Berowne's soliloquy at the beginning of this scene contrasts in its plainest of prose with the highly figurative verse of his previous self-communing at the end of Act III. There he complains that the boy-god on whom he has been exercising his whip has had his revenge by driving him to passionate poetry. Here he gleefully resumes the whip to punish 'hypocrisy', unaware that his own more sensational exposure is imminent. So confident is he that Rosaline has safely perused his lines that he boasts his loyalty to their oath, even accuses them of 'treason' – *he* rhyme or sigh or praise a pretty feature, the very idea! Nevertheless, his own 'treason' having come to light, it is he who is called upon to champion the humiliated sex, and with resounding hyperboles rally his warriors to win their ladies by some overwhelming entertainment.

coursing Hunting.

pitched a toil Set nets around a space (into which the quarry is driven).

pitch The black sticky substance which proverbially defiles. Pun on 'pitch', to set up. There is a possible echo of Berowne's description of Rosaline's eyes (III,1,192).

I the fool i.e. I am now the fool who says so. Is he echoing Costard's expression, 'sit thee down, sorrow' (I,1,305)?

Ajax A leading Greek in the Trojan War who, maddened by not being given the arms of the dead Hector, slaughtered a flock of sheep and then slew himself.

lie in my throat Tell a great lie.

the fool sent it i.e. himself.

God give him grace to groan! i.e. if only he will groan for love (which the King promptly does).

bird-bolt Blunt-headed arrow.

under the left pap At the heart.

The night of dew i.e. his tears.

as a coach i.e. each tear carries a picture of you in it.

do not love thyself . . . weep Instead of loving yourself, see your reflection in my tears and cause them to go on flowing (in order to be reflected in them).

shade folly Conceal my madness.

in thy likeness Addressed (but inaudibly) to the King.

a perjure One who has perjured himself, broken his oath.

wearing papers i.e. on his head as penalty for perjury. The crime was written on the paper.

In love, I hope The King hopes that Longaville's perjury is through falling in love, so keeping him company.

One drunkard Berowne overhears the King.

Am I the first . . . so? The embarrassment of a man who is swift to punish others (cf. I,1,126).

put thee in comfort i.e. by informing you of two others in like case (himself and the King).

not by two Not the first by two, i.e. the third.

the triumviry Comparing them to the Triumvirate, an alliance of three powerful rulers (Caesar, Pompey and Crassus), 60BC.

corner-cap Clerical cap with three or four corners.

the shape of Love's Tyburn The triangular shape of the gallows of Love that executes the simple-minded (Tyburn was London's place of execution at what is now the junction of Oxford Street and Edgware Road).

stubborn i.e. which have proved difficult to compose.

guards Ornamental trimmings.

Disfigure not his shop Do not deface his fashionable baggy hose (by tearing off the 'guards').

This same shall go He decides to keep to the verse (as if he had heard Berowne's remark).

A woman I forswore i.e. I vowed to have nothing to do with any woman.

Thy grace . . . disgrace in me i.e. your love, when won, absolves me of breaking my word.

exhal'st Dost cause to evaporate.

in thee it is It is absorbed in you.

To lose an oath to win a paradise i.e. to be perjured for love.

liver-vein Vein of love (of which the liver was then regarded as the seat).

makes flesh a deity Turns an ordinary human being into a goddess.

A green goose A young woman (cf. I,2,81).

amend us Put us right.

out o' th' way Off the right path (of their vows).

All hid Berowne uses the words of a children's game.

o'er-eye Look down on; 'in the sky' would suggest that Berowne's hiding-place is up a tree.

More sacks to the mill i.e. more work for Love the Executioner.

I have my wish Which he had uttered in l.17.

transformed Changed in character.

woodcocks Fools. The woodcock is easily caught and was often eaten in a dish.

coxcomb Fool (from the cap worn by a professional jester). 'Profane' is contrasted with 'divine', like 'earth' with 'heaven' in the next comment.

the wonder in a mortal eye! i.e. something to marvel at when beheld by a mere human.

Corporal Officer (i.e. servant of Love, the word Berowne applied to himself in III,1,182). Also a play on the word: corporal = of the human body.

Her amber hairs . . . quoted Her amber-coloured hair has caused amber itself to be criticized (written down) as dirty ('foul').

An amber-coloured raven . . . noted i.e. this observer (Dumain) has cleverly made note of a raven with *amber* plumage. A hit at Dumain for passing off his dark-haired lady as fair (the fashion). But in, V,2,42, Katharine attacks Rosaline for being a brunette, so perhaps here is only a pun on the raven being a 'fowl'.

Stoop Stooping.

with child i.e. her humped shoulder protrudes like a pregnant woman's stomach.

but then no sun must shine i.e. Dumain's love is only as fair as an overcast (dark) day.

Amen As if responding to the King's prayer ('good Lord').

a good word A pious expression.

will remember'd be i.e. I cannot put her out of my mind.

incision Blood-letting. A medieval practice still used in Elizabethan days for fevers. The blood would be collected in saucers.

misprision Obsolete legal term for 'mistake'.

ode Strictly, a poem of praise, and more elaborate than a lyric.

love can vary wit i.e. produce poems in different styles.

sonnet Originally any short lyrical poem, but later applied exclusively to the fourteen-line stanza (used by Berowne and Longaville).

alack Expressing regret, also pity.

velvet leaves i.e. the petals of the blossom.

Wished himself . . . breath Wished he could take the place of the wind.

thy cheeks may blow Suggested by the pictorial representation of winds as blown by puffed-out cheeks.

triumph so i.e. gain access to my love.

my hand is sworn i.e. I have taken a vow (the lover is now Dumain himself).

for youth unmeet Unsuited to young people.

Ethiop Dark-skinned Ethiopian. In comparison with you, Jupiter (an unfaithful husband) would describe his wife Juno thus.

deny himself for Jove Conceal his divinity.

more plain i.e. in simple prose.

fasting pain The pain of being made to abstain from love.

Ill, to example ill Wrong-doing by others, by setting a (bad) example to me (would provide an excuse for breaking my word).

a perjured note A paper attached to the head of a perjurer explaining his offence.

none offend . . . dote i.e. if all are guilty of 'doting', no one can be charged with the offence.

thy love is far from charity This contrasts the two emotions: physical passion ('love') and spiritual compassion ('charity'). He accuses Dumain of selfishly wishing to incriminate others ('society') as well.

I should blush The dramatic irony is that this severe critic of others is about to be exposed in his turn.

as his your case is such i.e. you are in exactly the same situation.

offending twice as much Because of his criticism of another.

You do not love Maria! For this vein of sarcasm (ironical use of the negative) he is about to get his (royal) deserts.

reek Rise like smoke. An uncomplimentary term.

for paradise To meet your love (Maria).

for your love i.e. for Katharine's sake.

faith infringed Double meaning of (1) the man who has sworn, and (2) the faith he has plighted and broken.

know so much by me i.e. be able to point the finger of scorn at me.

to whip hypocrisy An aside.

Good heart! what grace . . . in love? My good lover, what special dispensation have you been given to find fault with other lovers?

Your eyes do make no coaches Your eyes (*so you say now*) do not produce tears to carry the reflection of a beloved. This reference to the King's lyric tells him that he has been overheard.

no certain princess i.e. (there is, of course!) no such thing as a princess reflected in *your* eyes. This negative irony deliberately echoes that of the King at Longaville's expense.

You'll not be perjured Referring to I,1,297–8.

none but minstrels i.e. only paid entertainers.

like of sonneting i.e. are given to scribbling love lyrics.

are you not i.e. are you not ashamed (emphatic repetition).

o'ershot i.e. doing wrong by accusing each other. From shooting over and so missing the mark.

You found his mote . . . see You, Longaville, judged Dumain, then the King judged you.

a beam i.e. a much greater fault (in one who, not innocent himself, accuses another). From the New Testament parable of the man who finds a 'mote' in his brother's eye when he has a 'beam' (a large piece of timber) in his own. There is dramatic irony in Berowne's confident judgement on the others, as the audience knows that *his* love-letter is on its way to the King.

teen Grief.

gnat Caught in the 'eye-beam' of love.

Hercules The strong man in classical legend, reduced to whipping a 'gig' or top.

Solomon The wise King of the Jews, being so undignified as to accompany a rustic dance on the fiddle.

Nestor Greek leader in the Trojan War, reputed for his wisdom.

push-pin A child's game, played with pins, the object being to get a pin across an opponent's.

critic Timon An Athenian hater of his fellow-men, featured in Shakespeare's *Timon of Athens*.

laugh at idle toys Be amused by trifles.

caudle A warm, spiced drink for the sick (Quarto I and several editors). The better word is candle (Folio), called for by Berowne to pretend to search for their ailments; it is supported by 'over-view' in the next line, an unusual word for inspection.

moon-like As changeable as the moon.

groan for Joan Sigh for a woman. Used by Berowne at the end of his self-castigation in III,1,200.

pruning me Preening myself (making myself look smart, as a bird 'preens' its feathers).

state Standing posture (contrasted with 'gait', manner of walking).
Soft! Wait!
Whither away so fast? Berowne has seen Costard coming.
true Honest.
I post from love I hasten away from this company of lovers.
present A written petition being presented.
What makes treason here? What is treason doing here? A pun ready-made for Costard.
mar nothing Harm nothing. Often associated with 'make' in the phrase 'make or mar'.
go in peace away together i.e. two harmless things, Costard and his 'treason' are dismissed from his presence.
misdoubts Suspects.
Dun Adramadio Mispronunciation of Don Adriano de Armado (IV,1,88).
Why dost thou tear it? Speaking to Berowne, who has had time to recognize his own 'sonnet'.
needs not fear it i.e. there is no treason in it.
move him to passion i.e. make Berowne angry.
here is his name The signature detected by Holofernes in IV,2,131.
whoreson loggerhead Wretched thick-head.
mess The original number of people eating together in a group was four. Banquets were often arranged in fours, with one 'mess', or dish, for each group. The Services have improved on this!
and you, my liege Stressing the greater responsibility of the King as leader and initiator.
pick-purses in love i.e. lovers by stealth.
dismiss this audience Get rid of these rustics who must not hear my confession.
turtles Turtle-doves (love-birds). In the absence of Armado, Costard and Jaquenetta do not conceal their affection.
sirs Used as a general word for both sexes and lower ranks.
the true folk The not-so-simple Costard claims his love to be genuine in comparison with that of the oath-breakers. Some might be tempted to see this as a taunt by the lower class, just dismissed as 'sirs'.
As true we are We are as true. Contradicting Costard's 'traitors'?
an old decree A regulation imposed by the old (past their youth). He speaks as if it had not originated with the King.
cross the cause . . . born Run contrary to the impulse of love which leads to our being born.
of all hands In all our cases.
rent lines i.e. the torn-up sonnet. Either the King is finding it difficult to conceive of Berowne in love or is pretending amazement.
Inde Early name for India.
first op'ning . . . east Sunrise.
vassal head i.e. in subjection (as in 'obedient breast').
strooken blind i.e. eyes closed as if unable to bear the blaze.

Kisses the bare ground . . . breast This extreme expression suggests full prostration by an oriental.

peremptory Imperious, over-confident.

eagle-sighted Soaring high enough to be able to look directly at the sun; not the modern 'eagle-eyed'.

That is not blinded Better 'And is not blinded'. Similar faulty construction with 'That' in 1.218.

scarce seen a light Barely visible to the naked eye. The moon was then believed to have a satellite star.

the culled sovereignty The chosen best (like the short-list in a beauty competition, suggested by 'fair' in the next line).

several worthies make one dignity i.e. several distinct qualities combine to form one over-all excellence.

nothing wants . . . seek Nothing desired of man is lacking. Pun on 'want' (be lacking) and 'want' (desire).

the flourish of all gentle tongues The fine phrases of cultivated speech.

Fie, painted rhetoric! He immediately rounds on his own request (for artificial eloquence) as something unworthy.

things of sale Mere commercial goods.

passes Excels.

praise too short doth blot Inadequate praise is as worthless as a blot on paper.

five-score winters worn A centenarian.

varnish age as if new-born Give an old man (who looks at beauty) the sprightliness of renewed youth.

gives the crutch the cradle's infancy Rolls back the years from impotent old age to the nursery. Metonymy.

O', 'tis the sun . . . shine Rather like Armado, Berowne ends his most extravagant 'flourishes' with the plainest of terms.

By heaven An expression not of surprise but of emphasis.

black as ebony Inferior (in Elizabethan fashion) to fairness of hair. This criticism is taken by Berowne as a compliment; it may indeed have led to Rosaline's part in a modern performance being taken (effectively) by a black actress.

who can give an oath? Where is a book? Where is there an attorney before whom I can swear? Find me a book in which to write it down and sign it.

beauty doth beauty lack . . . look This could mean (1) a beautiful woman lacks appreciation of beauty if she does not use her eyes, or (2) a so-called beauty lacks essential beauty if she does not acquire a certain look in her eye, or (3) anybody else's guess!

paradox Calling a brunette 'fair' (beautiful).

school of night Possibly an allusion to a group of atheists patronized by Sir Walter Raleigh (see Introduction by R.W. David to the Arden Edition, pp.xxxvii to xli).

beauty's crest Fair hair worn on the head like a dazzling crest.

Devils soonest tempt . . . light i.e. devils who disguise themselves as angels succeed best.

decked Ornamented.

It mourns This act is a sign of mourning.

usurping hair False hair that 'usurps' the place of natural hair.

ravish doters with a false aspect Fascinate foolish admirers by means of a sham appearance.

to make black fair To convince people that 'black is beautiful'.

Her favour turns the fashion Her complexion (by example) changes the present fashion.

native blood is counted painting now Natural rosiness is regarded as put on (cosmetic).

avoid dispraise Escape such criticism.

Paints itself black i.e. on the eyebrows.

are chimney-sweepers black i.e. sweeps blacken themselves.

colliers counted bright Coalminers admired for their radiance.

crack Brag.

come in rain Walk out in wet weather.

colours i.e. the dyes in their hair.

I'll find a fairer face . . . today Today I will find a face, more beautiful than your lady's, that has not been washed to prove it.

talk till doomsday here Go on talking till the Day of Judgement where I am standing (as a penalty if I fail).

No devil i.e. after death he will find no devil (to fear as much as her).

vile stuff The teasers (in this kind of revenge on Berowne) are getting near the theme.

Look Pointing at his shoe.

my foot and her face i.e. my shoe and her complexion are of the same colour.

for such tread To tread on such coarse paving.

what upward lies Lies, such as her false colouring, seen by looking upward.

prove Our loving lawful . . . torn Prove that we can lawfully love our ladies and that we have not broken our solemn oath. Spoken as a challenge.

some flattery for this evil i.e. praise for having done wrong.

some authority how to proceed i.e. some legal backing for our future actions.

quillets An old and rare word for subtle distinctions at law. Possibly from *qu'il est*, the opening words of each clause in the case presented.

to cheat the devil i.e. to save us from punishment. One wonders who was likely to inflict it.

salve for perjury Remedy for the harm done by forswearing ourselves.

'tis more than need i.e. the remedy he offers is greater than is needed for a cure. The following speech is certainly longer than they expected!

affection's men-at-arms Love's warriors.

And where that . . . book These two lines are almost exactly repeated at
l.314: 'O, we have made a vow . . . books'. Similarly, the three lines,
'From women's eyes . . . Promethean fire' recur at l.346: 'From
women's eyes . . . academes'. The likeliest theory is that a first version,
'And where that . . . our learning there' (ll.292–313) was marked for
deletion, but the printer left it in, together with the second version, 'O
we have made . . . proves excellent' (ll.314–350). Most editors have
accepted both as 'undoubtedly Shakespeare'; the student might try to
judge for himself whether the second is an improvement on the first.

where that Whereas (stating the pre-condition).

in that Introducing what has actually happened.

the ground of study's excellence The foundation on which the best
kind of study is based.

Promethean fire i.e. inspiration. Prometheus, a legendary demi-god,
stole fire from heaven and introduced a number of arts to mankind.

universal plodding Reading laboriously in a variety of subjects.

poisons up Clogs with poison.

long-during Lasting a long time.

forsworn the use of eyes A piece of casuistry. Not to see a woman
means not to see at all, and so be unable to read the books which are
the reason for the vow not to see a woman.

adjunct Auxiliary or attachment.

in ladies' eyes i.e. the reflection (Berowne seems to be obsessed with
this idea).

Such fiery numbers Verse inspired by poetic fire.

keep the brain Keep to the brain.

barren practisers Those who work in such infertile soils as bookish
reading matter.

immured Imprisoned.

power Repetition of the same word at the end of two successive lines is
allowable in blank verse, but undesirable, except for unusual emphasis
(in this case triple). There is tautology in 'functions' and 'offices'.

gaze an eagle blind Outlast the piercing sight of an eagle.

When the suspicious head . . . stopped When the hearing of the most
circumspect of thieves can detect nothing.

sensible Susceptible to touch.

cockled Living in shells.

dainty Bacchus The god of wine, often represented as a beautiful but
effeminate youth.By comparison with Love's tongue (regarded as the
organ of taste and not speech) even his fastidious tastes seem coarse.

Hesperides One of Hercules's twelve Labours was to fetch the golden
apples of the goddess Juno from the garden where they were watched
over by three sisters, whose name, the Hesperides, is here given to the
garden.

Subtle Cunning. The Sphinx, a composite monster with the head of a
woman, posed difficult riddles to its intended victims.

Apollo's lute The favourite instrument of the god of music was the lyre, not the lute (brought to Europe from the East by the Crusaders). Apollo was represented as a handsome young man with a fine head of hair.

the voice of all the gods . . . harmony i.e. it is as if the gods, all speaking together, soothed the heavens with the harmony (here melody) of their voices.

temper'd i.e. brought to the right condition (for composition) by mixture.

Else none . . . excellent i.e. without them (women's eyes) no one excels in anything at all.

keeping what is sworn i.e. *if* you keep your oaths.

a word that loves all men A meaningless transposition of the words in the previous line.

the authors of these women (?) the begetters.

by whom we men are men i.e. through birth.

to find ourselves i.e. through love.

religion to be thus forsworn A paradoxical expression, as 'religion' was first associated with binding vows.

fulfils the law 'He that loveth another hath fulfilled the law' (Romans 13,8).

Saint Cupid Like the battle-cry of 'St George!'

Pell-mell i.e. advance in a mad headlong rush.

get the sun of them Face them when the sun is in their eyes (so neutralizing their eye-beams).

to plain-dealing i.e. in simple language instead of the military metaphors ('glozes' are emblematic expressions).

Forerun Run in front of, as in a procession.

No time shall be omitted . . . time An obscure sentence unless 'time' is treated like its twin, 'tide' ('betide' means happen); no time will be wasted that will pass before the event.

be fitted Be suitably spent.

Allons! Let's go (French).

Sowed cockle Weed sown instead of corn.

in equal measure i.e. dispensing judgement to all.

Light wenches may prove plagues Flighty girls may be our punishment.

our copper buys no better treasure i.e. our base behaviour (in breaking our oaths) deserves no better reward.

Revision questions on Act IV

1 The main action in each of the three scenes results from the wrong delivery or unintended overhearing of love messages. What is the result in each case?

2 Comment on the differing functions of prose and verse (rhymed and unrhymed) as exemplified in this Act.

3 Describe the parts played in this Act by (a) the Princess and (b) the King.

Act V Scene 1

The two sets of comic characters have their first meeting in the final act. After Moth, like a precocious schoolboy, has baited schoolmaster Holofernes, Armado announces that the King has called on him for some entertainment for the visitors and asks for help.

Holofernes promptly suggests the presentation of that ever popular group, the 'Nine Worthies' of the ancient world. A preliminary casting – of Costard as Pompey the Great, because of his physical size, and Moth as Hercules in the infant state in which he strangled serpents – reveals a shortage of actors which can only be supplied by doubling or even trebling parts. The slow-witted constable cannot do more than volunteer to join in some rustic dancing (a performance prevented by events).

Commentary

In all this welter of Latin tags, obscure puns, meaningless abstractions and artificial epithets (surely not exceeded in this by any other scene in the whole spectrum of Shakespeare's stage productions) a contemporary audience will have found (or pretended to find) more amusement than today's painstaking student does! Apart from such exaggerated characterization, its chief purpose must be to arouse anticipation of the ensuing farce, as happens with the later more comically effective parallel of 'Pyramus and Thisbe' in *A Midsummer Night's Dream*.

Satis quod sufficit What is sufficient is enough (this Scene is full of Latin expressions). The Folio *quid* must be a misprint.
Your reasons Your discourse.
sententious Full of good sense.
pleasant without scurrility A point insisted on by the Parson in IV,2,52.
affection Affectation.
audacious Bold (in a good sense).
opinion Dogmatism.
strange without heresy Original without offending against accepted beliefs.

this quondam day This day *which has passed*. Probably Act V takes place on the following day; on the other hand *quondam*, in the sense of 'former', had become a Latin tag. The Parson probably means nothing more than 'this very day'.

Novi hominem tanquam te I know the man as well as I do you (Latin).

peremptory Masterful.

his tongue filed His expression polished.

vain, ridiculous, and thrasonical This comes as somewhat of an anti-climax to the string of praises. 'Thrasonical' was an Elizabethan term for 'boastful', from Thraso, a bragging soldier in Terence's play *Eunuchus*.

picked Carefully preened, i.e. excessively refined in appearance.

peregrinate Elizabethan word for 'looking like some traveller with affectations acquired abroad'. Nathaniel regards it as a 'singular' (outstanding) addition to his vocabulary.

table-book Tablet. The word 'draw' (amended by some to 'draws') could be the imperative often used in stage directions.

He draweth out . . . argument He spins his words out at such length that the meaning cannot keep up with them. 'Staple' (a word of several meanings) probably refers to the quality of the fibre composing the thread.

fanatical phantasimes Extravagantly fanciful people.

insociable and point-devise companions Uncongenial and (when encountered and conversed with) scrupulously precise persons.

rackers of orthography Abusers of the rules of spelling (from the 'rack' on which victims of torture were stretched).

dout . . . det The 'b' was dropped in spelling as well as pronunciation, until restored by pedants who probably affectedly pronounced it. Holofernes insists on sounding the silent 'b' and 'l'.

clepeth Calls (archaic, as in the poetic 'yclept').

cauf Pronunciation transitional to modern 'cahf'.

vocatur Is called (Latin).

nebor i.e. the guttural is silent; but 'neigh' is not of the same origin as 'neighbour'.

This is abhominable i.e. this sort of pronunciation is abominable. Here the Pedant is himself guilty of error in this contemporary example of false analogy, regarding 'abominable' (from the Latin for 'ill-omened', ab omine) as derived from *ab homine*, in the sense of 'inhuman'. In the Folio the 'h' is printed in both pronunciations.

It insinuateth me of insanie To me it suggests insanity.

Ne intellegis domine? Don't you understand, sir?

Laus Deo, bone intelligo Praise be to God, I understand quite well. In view of Holofernes's discreet reference to Nathaniel's error in the next line, the correct adverb *bene* is best replaced by *bone*, which the Pedant gently ridicules by turning it into French, *fort bon*, very good.

Priscian Priscianus was a Roman teacher in Constantinople c. AD525. Some grammatical works of his have survived.

a little scratched Slightly damaged.

Videsne quis venit? Do you see who is coming?

Video, et gaudeo I see and rejoice.

Chirrah! An affected pronunciation of 'sirrah', used to offending servants or naughty boys. Here addressed to Moth, who is probably playing some trick.

Quare Why?

Men of peace Condescendingly addressing mere civilians. The distinction is recognized in Holofernes's greeting, 'Most military sir'.

alms-basket Used for collecting scraps to be given to the poor.

honorificabilitudinitatibus This 'longest word', created from a string of tacked-on suffixes, has been recorded in various forms down the centuries. It has a rival in a Welsh railway station.

flapdragon A raisin snatched from burning brandy and swallowed whole.

peal Loud series of changes on a 'peal' of church bells.

Monsieur Speaking to Holofernes.

lettered i.e. a man of letters, a scholar.

the horn-book School primer consisting of a parchment inscribed with the alphabet and digits, and covered with horn, which was transparent.

pueritia Boyhood. His first encounter with Armado's page.

most silly sheep Moth has got him to say 'Baa'.

Quis Who (is the sheep?) The Latin interrogative pronoun.

thou consonant i.e. a voiceless sound by itself, therefore nothing.

the five vowels Suggested by Holofernes's use of 'consonant'. The last and the fifth is 'u', to which Moth is leading him on.

The sheep i.e. the 'i' uttered by Holofernes.

o, u i.e. oh, you. A final confirmation that the Pedant is a sheep.

sweet touch Clever stroke.

venue A hit in fencing.

which is wit-old Whose wits have decayed. A 'wittol' could be either a half-wit or a contented 'cuckold', symbolically represented with horns on his brows. Applied to Holofernes this seems absurd.

What is the figure? What figure of speech are you using?

gig Top. Suitable employment for an 'infant'. Could be made of horn.

your infamy Your reputation (as a cuckold?).

manu cita With a swift hand. This meaningless Latin phrase has had various acrostic-type emendations: *unciatim* by twelfths, i.e. little by little; and Theobald's *circum-circa*, round and round, which is used in the *Globe* edition.

gingerbread Preserved ginger.

remuneration i.e. only three-farthings, the coin given him by Armado for carrying his letter.

halfpenny purse This was a small purse for halfpennies only.

pigeon-egg i.e. a small one.

discretion Wisdom.

my bastard My son, born out of wedlock.

ad dunghill The peasant's mistake is due to the attraction of 'd' from preposition to noun in *ad unguem*, Latin phrase meaning 'to a nail', or in English idiom, 'to a hair'. The fingernail was used to detect flaws in marble.

smell Double meaning!

Arts-man, perambulate My dear scholar, walk on ahead (and away from the 'barbarous'). Cf. modern 'preamble', introductory remarks.

singled Separated.

charge-house School, where a small fee was charged or paid by the parish. The word is not found elsewhere, so it may be 'church-house', where village children were often educated. There was a village school on Harrow Hill in Shakespeare's day. The Spaniard would be more used to mountains!

congratulate Salute (obsolete).

the posteriors The latter part.

rude multitude Ignorant majority.

liable Suitable (in the sense of fulfilling an obligation), as also 'congruent' (acting in harmony) and 'measurable' (befitting), all three used to say that 'posteriors' is a good word for 'afternoon'.

my familiar My close friend.

inward between us Shared in confidence.

remember thy courtesy Perhaps Armado is reminding Holofernes to show customary respect for the sovereign by removing his hat at the mention of his name, and then telling him to replace it.

importunate Urgent.

designs Plans.

but let that pass He pretends to pull himself up before betraying the royal confidence to a stranger.

dally with my excrement i.e. play with the hair (excrescence) which grows (Latin *crescere*, to grow) on my upper lip.

recount no fable Tell no falsehood.

The very all of all The essence of what I have to say.

delightful ostentation Display affording delight (to the spectators).

antic Grotesque performance.

firework Firework display.

eruptions Outbursts, amusing inventions.

to the end to crave With the purpose of asking.

the Nine Worthies Traditionally in three groups: Classical – Hector, Alexander, Julius Caesar; Jewish – Joshua, David, Judas Maccabaeus; Christian – Arthur, Charlemagne, Godfrey of Bouillon. But alterations were made to suit the occasion: here Hercules and Pompey are added.

Sir . . . Sir The first is addressed to Armado (who will make the introduction); the second must be to Nathaniel (the Folio unaccountably has 'Sir Holofernes').

as concerning some entertainment of time About a performance of some duration?

assistance Presence as helpers.

illustrate Illustrious.

present Impersonate.

myself; and this gallant gentleman, Judas Maccabaeus Possibly the Pedant is thinking of Judas (a Jewish, not a classical, hero) as two persons. Or there is another misprint.

He is not quantity enough There is not enough of him.

Shall I have audience? Will you listen? (A schoolmaster's impatience of interruption).

in minority Under age. Here, infancy.

strangling a snake Hercules, son of Jupiter and Alcmena, when barely eight months old strangled two snakes sent by the jealous Juno to destroy him.

apology Justification. Not the modern 'excuse for an offence'.

hiss The common expression of an audience's disapproval of a bad performance. A mocking suggestion by Moth that the author can thus get his own back on his critics.

to make an offence gracious To turn a rude comment (the hissing) into a fortunate coincidence (the provision of 'sound effects').

have the grace Are lucky enough.

I will play three myself For such self-confidence. cf. *A Midsummer Night's Dream* I,2, where Bottom volunteers for three parts in turn.

Thrice-worthy The three parts are an excuse for a sarcastic use of 'thrice' meaning 'extremely'. Cf. the poetical 'thrice-happy'.

fadge Succeed.

Via An exclamation, like 'come along!' (Italian).

tabor Small drum, played usually with one hand, together with a pipe.

the hay A country dance in which the performers wind in and out.

Act V Scene 2

The Princess and her ladies compare their respective lovers' favours, their mockery of the men interwoven with a strand of feminine rivalry between the brunette Rosaline and the blonde Katharine. Boyet announces the arrival of a quartet of befurred Russians who, he explains, are really the King and his courtiers, whom he has (accidentally) overheard planning the venture with uproarious mirth. The Princess suggests an exchange of love-tokens, to baffle their admirers.

Heralded by Moth (appearing, it must be supposed, by permission of the Worthies), who is as much put out of his part by Berowne's prompting as by Boyet's teasing, the lovers approach the wrong ladies. Rosaline (as the Princess) leads the King a dance with her swift changes of mood; then each couple (wrongly paired) in turn 'converse apart' after a brief dialogue, remarkable only for atrocious puns. Finally Rosaline briskly dismisses the 'Muscovites'.

After the ladies have told each other of the declarations of love received, Rosaline advises them to mock the men still further by ridiculing to their faces the absurd behaviour of the previous visitors. They depart, leaving Boyet to meet the King and offer to fetch the ladies. In his absence Berowne mockingly portrays him as the supreme example of the affected courtier, a description immediately given flesh and blood by the extravagant gestures of Boyet when he returns, ushering in the ladies.

The King bluntly invites them to reside in the Court instead of their humbler accommodation in pavilions in the park, but the Princess declines, if only to save the men from the disgrace of oath-breaking. Besides, they have not been (as he would appear to think) left to their own devices: they have been kept amused by some Russians, whom Rosaline boldly characterizes as talkative idiots. A sudden exchange of wit between her and Berowne leads to the revelation that the ladies had prior knowledge of the masking. While the King is crestfallen, Berowne makes an eloquent profession to Rosaline of his conversion from high-flown terms to the humblest speech. Worsted in his argument with her, he calls on the others to make their own excuses. The King responds and is decoyed by the Princess into swearing that he will not reject the lady to whom (as a Russian) he has professed love: he is dismayed to find that the lady wearing his favour then was not the Princess, but Rosaline. When the Princess, in turn, challenges Berowne, the latter upbraids the ladies for the trick they have played and scoffs at Boyet for his part in it, in a long, 'Berownic' harangue.

A fortunate distraction arrives in the form of the Worthies, who are successively barracked. Armado first presents the King with the *dramatis personae,* in order of appearance:

Pompey: Costard the Clown.
Alexander: Nathaniel the Curate.
Hercules (infant)*:* Moth the Page.
Judas Maccabaeus: Holofernes the Pedant.
Hector: Armado the Braggart.

The same actors were to present in a second appearance the remaining Worthies, but the harassed 'Hector' is suddenly accused by 'Pompey' (some editors insert directions indicating that Berowne is the informer) of having made Jaquenetta pregnant. The subsequent un-Worthy brawl is suddenly halted by the news of the death of the Princess's father.

She decides on immediate departure, from which the King seeks to dissuade her, while Berowne makes an eloquent plea that their fourfold state of love is due to the fascination exercised on them by the ladies themselves. The Princess, after demurely rebuking the four for making a merry pastime of their love, promises that, if the King spends the ensuing year in a lonely hermitage for her sake, she will be his at the end of the period.

Katharine and Maria make similar promises and, as a climax, Rosaline imposes on the talkative mocker Berowne a year's round of visits to sickbeds. Their 'Labour of Love' is 'Lost', but only for a while. The solemn prospect in front of the four gallants is given some relief by the return of the chastened Worthies (and others?) to sing the 'dialogue' of Cuckoo (for Spring) and Owl (for Winter) in two of Shakespeare's best-known lyrics.

Commentary

The dialogue between the lords and ladies in this long scene brings their complicated courtship to an inconclusive end. The audience finds more entertainment in the keenly anticipated parade of Worthies. This is much inferior to that other village performance, 'Pyramus and Thisbe' in *A Midsummer Night's Dream*, in having no plot. It rouses much-needed laughter, until the twin 'catastrophes' (a Greek word for the last and fatal turn in a drama) have a sobering effect: Jacquenetta's pregnancy and the news of the death of the French King.

The Nine Worthies (from many ages and parts of the world) were once as familiar as country dancing; their busts in niches may still be seen in parks like that of Stowe in Buckinghamshire. Nine has long been a magic number, especially in the form of three times three. 1593 is the date on the Rushton Triangular Lodge in Northamptonshire, with every feature in threes, symbolic of the Trinity, and its digits add up to 18. The references to three and its multiples, as well as the triads of Armado (I,2,157 and IV,1,61) and Berowne (IV,3,15 and III,1,195) are conspicuous in this play. In the entertainment given in V,2 the numbers were, however, incomplete.

fairings Gifts purchased at fairs.

walled about with diamonds This may refer to herself, perhaps receiving a coronet from the King; or it may be a figure set in diamonds.

as much love in rhyme . . . and all i.e. the King has produced a miniature poem on a minute sheet of paper (easier to hide?). The intricate rhymes of the sonnet (here sixteen lines) make it a gem for size among poems.

fain to seal on Cupid's name Pleased to attach a wax seal to, with Cupid's name on it.

wax Pun on (1) the wax of the seal, and (2) the old word meaning 'to grow', here 'to grow up'.

five thousand year i.e. since the days of the early gods.

shrewd unhappy gallows Accursed scoundrel (gallows-bird), the cause of unhappiness in others.

light, like you Light-hearted, as you are.

dark meaning Hidden significance. There is a pun on 'light' (not serious) and 'light' (not dark).

mouse Term of endearment.

A light condition . . . dark i.e. frivolity in a brunette.

more light i.e. your meaning is not yet clear (a candle is suggested).

taking it in snuff i.e. being offended by it (i.e. my meaning). Pun on this sense and actually 'snuffing' a candle: 'mar (spoil) the light' and 'darkly' in the dark, after the candle is out.

still i' th' dark i.e. always furtively.

light wench Irresponsible woman.

I weigh not you Either (1) I weigh less than you (and therefore am 'light') or (2) I attach no weight (and therefore no value) to you or what you say.

that's you care not That's because you care not.

Great reason i.e. for not valuing you.

past care is still past cure Inverted form of 'what is past cure is past caring about', to answer Katharine's 'care not'.

Well bandied Well exchanged, as in a tennis rally ('a set of wit').

The numbers true i.e. the metre is correct (cf. 'numbers ratified', IV,2,117).

the numb'ring The calculation (twenty thousand).

drawn my picture i.e. in words.

Much in the letters In answer to the Princess's question, Rosaline probably suggests that the only resemblance to her is in the blackness of the letters. This the Princess turns into an unflattering comparison.

Fair as a text B Beautiful as a big black manuscript capital letter B.

'Ware pencils, ho! A danger warning – pencils are being used as weapons.

red dominical In early almanacs the days January 1 to 7 were denoted by the letters A to G. The letter for Sunday (dominical) was printed in red.

golden letter A reference to Katharine's fair hair.

your face . . . O's Spots!

A pox of Exclamation, from the 'pox', any disease with spots on the skin.

beshrew all shrows Curse all vicious tongues. Some editors transfer this line, with its strong language, to Katharine, the object of this attack.

twain Two. To rhyme with Dumain; or, one glove by itself might be a challenge.

translation of hypocrisy Rendering in words of feelings that are not genuine.

Vilely compil'd, profound simplicity Wretchedly composed, a downright piece of ignorance.

I think no less i.e. I agree it is too long.

might never part i.e. might remain clasped together, holding the pearls.

to purchase mocking so To make such presents only to be mocked at.

in by th' week i.e. caught temporarily in love. Possibly from service or imprisonment by the week.

wait the season i.e. not anticipate the right time; the same as 'observe the times'.

bootless rhymes Verse written in vain.

hests Commands.

make him proud . . . jests Cause him to take pride in offering the praise that would make me proud, were I not playing a trick.

Pair-Taunt like Like a 'pertaunt', which has been recorded in no English dictionary and has been variously emended to: pedant, pageant, portent or potent. See the explanation of this word as a winning hand of four cards of a sort (e.g. four Kings, Aces etc.) in the Arden Edition by R.W. David, p.130.

his fate Not his future wife, but the power controlling his destiny.

Folly, in wisdom hatched . . . fool His lover-folly, because it has grown out of previous wisdom, bears still the outward stamp of intellect, speaks in a scholarly fashion, and indulges in witty sallies, all of which give some charm to what is after all a fool in love, for all his learning.

gravity's revolt to wantonness i.e. a reversion from responsibility to irresponsible behaviour.

Since all the power . . . simplicity i.e. since it (folly in the wise) uses all the resources of its intellect to demonstrate there is something to be admired in such foolishness.

Encounters mounted are Attacks are prepared.

Saint Denis to Saint Cupid! Rival war cries, St Denis being the patron saint of France, while Cupid is a mock 'saint' invoked by – how did she guess? – the King.

charge their breath The metaphor of loaded cannon extends that of 'Armed in arguments'.

scout Addressing Boyet as if he had been sent on a military reconnaissance.

addrest Making their way.

a pretty knavish page i.e. Moth.

conned his embassage Learned by heart the message he is to deliver.

made a doubt Expressed a fear.

rubbed his elbow A sign of satisfaction.

fleered Grinned.

turned on the toe Turned round to leave.

passion's solemn tears Sarcastic: this is their way of sighing for love.

Muscovites This may have been suggested by a contemporary play or masque featuring fur-clad visitors from Russia, then becoming better known through trade.

love-feat Love-suit.

Unto his several mistress . . . several An ungrammatical passage: each to his own mistress, whom he will recognize by his distinctive present.

tasked Put to the test.

grace Favour, fortune.

Despite of suit i.e. however much he pleads.

change you favours too Speaking to Katharine and Maria.

removes Exchanges.

most in sight Conspicuously.

to cross theirs To thwart their intention.

in mocking merriment She has taken Boyet's account of their antics seriously.

several counsels Individual professions of love.

with visages displayed i.e. unmasked.

their penned speech i.e. Moth's introduction, which he has had to learn.

kill the speaker's heart i.e. dishearten him.

come in if he be out Prompt him if he forgets his words (or, rather, theirs).

no such sport . . . o'erthrown i.e. nothing so enjoyable as someone else's stratagem defeated by your own.

To make theirs ours . . . our own i.e. to borrow their trick of disguising their real identities (by exchanging favours) and then yield nothing in return.

stay i.e. as victors on the battlefield.

mocking intended game i.e. laughing at the fun they hoped to have.

Blackamoors Probably actors with their faces blacked. Negroes were popular figures in masques, though here they are scarcely compatible with heavily befurred Russians.

taffeta A thin fabric (then probably silk) used to make the masks. Boyet means the ladies' beauty is invisible.

holy parcel Sacred group; 'parcel' in this sense is now debased.

Out of your favours By your kindness.

brings me out Makes me forget my lines.

perfectness Berowne's presumed coaching of Moth has not made him word perfect. The shrewd Rosaline detects the authorship in l.305!

What would these strangers? Speaking as the Princess.

some plain man i.e. the elaborate introduction is as incomprehensible as Russian!

Know what they would Enquire the purpose of their visit.

gentle visitation A visit paid out of courtesy (in spite of our outlandish garb).

a measure A stately kind of dance

They say Boyet solemnly pretends to translate.

It is not so This is not true. She takes the word 'measure' in the first sense. If they have 'measured' many miles they will know the answer, if not in inches, then in 'weary steps'.

We numbering nothing . . . you A neat rejoinder; what is done out of love is not reckoned up.

without accompt Without counting the cost.

show the sunshine i.e. remove your masks.

like savages i.e. like heathens (who worship the sun).

but a moon i.e. with the pallor that brunettes often have; or as a reflection of the Princess.

clouded i.e. masked.

Blessed Because of their contact with the ladies' eyes.

these thy stars i.e. the ladies in attendance.

watery eyne Tearful eyes (archaic form of the plural).

but moonshine in the water Something insubstantial: the reflection of our faces in the water of your tears. The vain petitioner must ask for something better.

vouchsafe one change i.e. grant only one turn (in the dance) – the limited request of a 'beggar'.

not strange Not a foreign custom.

Not yet? The musicians have not been quick enough to strike up.

vouchsafe some motion to it Condescend to dance some steps to it.

Our ears vouchsafe it i.e. they follow the rhythm.

nice Over-particular.

take hands:— we will not dance A second teasing action, proffering their hands and then refusing to dance.

Curtsy, sweet hearts Calling on the others to join her in bidding the strangers farewell.

More measure of this measure! More steps in this dance!

We can afford no more . . . price i.e. we cannot go on selling so cheaply.

Price you yourselves i.e. name your price.

Your absence only The only sum that will buy their *presence*!

half once to you i.e. less respect for the man behind the mask.

two treys Two threes at dice. Berowne offers to throw up another three. The game, of course, is imaginary.

an if you grow so nice If you are going to be so precise.

Metheglin A Welsh drink, made from honey.

wort An infusion of malt in a sweet state before fermenting into beer.

malmsey Wine.

Seventh sweet Addressed to Berowne himself!

cog Cheat in throwing the dice.

grievest my gall Hurtest my sore place (caused by constant irritation); but 'gall' is also a bitter growth on an oak tree, and so the opposite of 'sweet'.

Therefore meet i.e. suitable for two opponents, who should be bitter to each other. This mixture of forced rhymes and far-fetched puns would have tested the best-educated Elizabethan in the audience.

Please it you If you please (French construction).

As much in private i.e. say as much again between ourselves.

afford my speechless visor half Supply me with a tongue, i.e. half of your two (her mask having a false tongue to keep it in position).

Veal As a Dutchman (a foreigner to the French) would understand 'ville', the end of her lover's name (if he spoke English!).

a fair lord calf Adding to the Longaville's puzzlement at this bovine interpretation by declaring that the calf is masculine.

part Go shares in.

your half i.e. your wife (cf. 'better half'). An unaspirated 'alf' may be considered a part of 'calf'.

Take all and wean it Take the whole animal and rear it.

an ox A fool (obsolete).

you butt yourself You are hurting yourself.

give horns i.e. be unfaithful to your (future) husband.

Above the sense of sense Beyond the capacity of ordinary reason to grasp their meaning. The intellectual content of these witty exchanges has certainly reached vanishing point.

so sensible Seemeth their conference Their conversation seems so acutely perceptive.

their conceits have wings Their ingenious ideas flash past.

dry-beaten with pure scoff! Bloodlessly defeated by sheer mockery.

simple wits This could mean anything from artlessness to stupidity. Is it a parting shot, wittily countered by the Princess's reference to the (frozen) climate from which the visitors would appear to have come?

Tapers Mere candle-lights, easily snuffed out.

Well-liking (Strictly of the body) 'plump and well-fed'. Indicative of little brain.

kingly-poor flout! A poor attempt to mock us, even though they had a King among them!

but in visors Except masked.

pert Smart.

weeping-ripe On the point of weeping (in his search for a word).

out of all suit i.e. until he had no more service he could offer.

No point The French negative, *point*, was used in a similar pun in II,1,89.

Qualm Passing feeling of sickness.

plain statute-caps Statutory caps (of wool) worn by apprentices.

digest this harsh indignity i.e. swallow this mocking attack on their pride.

lame with blows i.e. wounded by your words.

change favours i.e. exchange (back again) their lovers' gifts (the Princess with Rosaline, Katharine with Maria).

repair Return.

Blow like sweet roses i.e. blossom with your natural complexions when you are unmasked.

commixture Complexion.

vailing clouds Lowering the clouds (which had previously hidden their brightness).

blown i.e. in full bloom, not (as today) having lost their petals.

Avaunt, perplexity! Begone, puzzlement! i.e. the masks that baffle. Or is she dismissing Boyet's artificial phrasing? He is about to be diagnosed in detail by Berowne.

as well known as disguised As much in their familiar apparel as when they were dressed up.

shapeless gear Clumsy clothing.

rough carriage so ridiculous Such an absurdly uncouth bearing.

Whip Move quickly.

land In its old meaning of a 'stretch of grass-covered ground', or just a rhyming word?

pecks up wit Collects clever phrases.

When God doth please i.e. with no preconceived purpose.

wakes Local festivals.

wassails Seasonal drinking parties.

that sell by gross i.e. the wholesalers who have no contact with the buyers, nor possess the 'grace' (the arts of persuasion) to attract them. Probably suggested by 'retails' in l.317 above.

pins the wenches on his sleeve i.e. he controls them as if they were his property, and flaunts his conquests.

carve i.e. choose for himself (rare); make a proposal to a lady.

lisp Speak in an affected manner.

the ape of form The sedulous follower of fashion.

monsieur the nice The gentleman of refinement.

tables Backgammon.

mean Middle part, tenor.

in ushering In proceeding before and introducing a person of importance.

Mend him who can Let anyone improve on his performance if he can.

whale his bone A frequent comparison, though the ivory tusks of the walrus were then the commodity.

that will not die in debt Who must pay their due.

the due of i.e. in the flattering term of.

See where it comes! A disrespectful reference to Boyet and his absurd gesturing.

Behaviour, what wert thou . . . now? Suggesting there was a more natural kind of graceful bearing until Boyet cheapened it.

Fair in all hail is foul A pun: the greeting 'fair time of day' when it is *hailing* should be 'foul time of day'.

Construe my speeches better i.e. better than in your opening remark.

if you may If you can.

to our court i.e. to the King's palace from the pavilions in the park.

hold your vow Enable you to keep your word.

that which you provoke i.e. the breaking of my vow to which you provoked me by your beauty.

virtue (Magic) power.

nickname Name falsely, i.e. there is no 'virtue' (used here in the sense of 'goodness') in such seduction.

office Function.

a breaking cause A cause of breaking (oaths).

desolation Solitude (obsolete).

unvisited Pretending ignorance of the 'Russians'.

pleasant game Pleasing entertainment.

to the manner of the days According to the prevailing fashion.

fools would fain have drink An indirect way of calling the Russians fools.

dry to me Barren in my view. Based on Rosaline's 'thirsty'.

greet With eyes best seeing heaven's fiery eye Pay our addresses, when our vision is at its best, to the blazing sun.

By light we lose light We are dazzled into temporary blindness.

Your capacity The extent of your knowledge. He means that Rosaline can afford to treat valuable things as trifles.

proves Her hint that by his argument he seems a 'poor fool' to her is taken up by Berowne before she can utter it.

It were a fault i.e. it would be wrong (to snatch, were it not that what you snatch is yours).

that visor Not pointing to the mask, which, of course, Berowne has not brought with him, but using it to taunt him with having a face worse than that which covered it.

that superfluous case In other words, the mask failed to disguise the wearer.

Hold his brows! i.e. hold his head up.

plagues Literally (1) the King's apparent sickness, and figuratively (2) Rosaline's wit.

for perjury (Punishment) for either (1) breaking the oaths made in Act I, or (2) their recent false disguises.

Can any face of brass . . . out? i.e. it is useless for us to *brazen* it out any longer (that we know nothing about the Russians). Berowne then offers himself for punishment for forsaking plain speech.

flout Scornful remark.

keen conceit Sharp-edged wit.

wish thee never more Never again ask you.

wait Call upon (you); 'will I' is understood.

the motion The power to move (in feeling). For 'speeches penn'd' see 'vilely penned', l.305.

a blind harper's song A tune by one of those unfortunates who can only fiddle for a living.

Taffeta phrases Elaborate expressions. Cf. the literal use of taffeta in l.159.

precise Fastidiously correct.

Three-pil'd Trebly thick, like the 'hair' of a rich carpet.

hyperboles Poetical exaggerations (a figure of speech).

spruce affection Affected artificiality (tautology).

blown me full of maggot ostentation i.e. (metaphorically) made me appear disgustingly pretentious (cf. 'fly-blown').

God knows Because the hand is hidden within the glove.

russet yeas . . . noes i.e.plain 'yes' and 'no', as from the simple wearers of coarse woollen garments (russets and kerseys).

sans crack or flaw Without an accidental crack or a fault in the making.

Sans 'sans' Berowne has slipped back into 'ostentation'.

Yet I have a trick . . . rage i.e. I am still liable to show a symptom of the old disease ('old' because I am now recovering from it).

'Lord have mercy on us' The pathetic notice placed on the doors of those stricken with the plague.

visited Afflicted by the plague.

you are not free i.e. you are also infected.

the Lord's tokens i.e. plague spots (fatal signs). Put on the tokens worn by the ladies.

they are free They are not infected (i.e. not really in love).

Our states are forfeit . . . undo us i.e. far from being free, we have been condemned and fined to the extent of all our property; do not ruin us.

That you stand forfeit . . . that sue By punning on 'sue' (1) to pay court to ladies and (2) to prosecute in court, Rosaline declares they cannot be both condemned men and prosecutors.

Speak for yourselves Turning to his companions, for whom he has so far been the (unavailing) spokesman.

rude transgression Clumsy offence, i.e. the 'Russian' intrusion.

Your oath once broke . . . forswear Having broken an oath once, you no longer attach importance to oath-breaking.

this oath of mine i.e. not to reject the lady to whom he spoke.

I will i.e. I will despise you if you break it.

God give thee joy of him Spoken sarcastically of an ill-fitting partner for life.

this jewel did she wear i.e. after the exchange.

your pearl again i.e. the pearl sent to Rosaline by Berowne and given the Princess in exchange for the King's jewel. The Princess is addressing Berowne in this line.

Neither of either Pleonasm for 'neither the one nor the other', a form of emphasis repeated in 'both twain'.

remit Surrender my right to.

consent Concerted plan.

our merriment Our improvised entertainment.

dash Spoil.

please-man One who is always ready to oblige.

slight zany Worthless mountebank.

mumble-news Gossip.

trencher-knight One who acquits himself well at mealtimes.

Dick Fellow. Used contemptuously.

smiles his cheek in years Wrinkles his face (like an old man's) with laughter.

Told our intents before i.e. betrayed our plans.

the sign of she i.e. the favour each gave his mistress.

in will and error i.e. by choice and by mistake.

Much upon this 'tis This is what it practically amounts to.

And might not you And was it not you that were able to. Identifying the 'carry-tale'.

by the square By measuring its length.

upon the apple of her eye i.e. so close that you are reflected in the pupil.

trencher Platter from which food is served (but not here the one held by a man-servant).

allow'd Licenced (to play the clown professionally).

smock A female garment. Metonymy for 'Women will be the death of you'.

leaden sword Mock weapon, like those used on the stage.

manage Piece of horsemanship.

career Charge (the length of the lists).

tilting straight i.e. already on horse-back.

pure wit A sarcastic welcome to the clown's muddled mind as a change from the sort of contest he has been taking part in.

O Lord, sir But indeed, sir.

pursents Mispronunciation of 'presents', impersonates.

under correction The legal 'with respect'. Costard has a habit of contradicting himself.

beg us i.e. make fools of us. The full expression would be: 'You cannot beg guardianship of us (a profitable undertaking then) as mentally handicapped heirs, from the Court of Awards'. One test of an idiot was to see if he could count.

whereuntil it doth amount What it comes to. This may refer to (1) a total sum, or (2) the result of some performance (i.e. the kind of entertainment the court is going to get).

by reckoning As a tapster! (I,2,38).

parfect Costard's mistake for 'perform', possibly with the contrast of 'perfect' and 'poor' in mind.

Pompion Pumpkin, a word used of a very large man. He goes on to speak of himself as Pompey, so there must be a play here on his size.

shame-proof i.e. after their oath-breaking and the Russian fiasco they cannot further be touched by a sense of shame.

That sport best pleases . . . how i.e. the worst amateurish effort gives the most pleasure (by its attempt to please). Cf. the similar opinion of Theseus in *A Midsummer Night's Dream*, V,1,82.

Where zeal strives . . . presents i.e. in which case their enthusiasm does its best to satisfy the audience, with the result that what meaning the play has is lost in the eager antics with which it is performed.

that which it presents Him who acts it.

Their form confounded . . . mirth i.e. the shapeless form taken by a play in their hands can produce nothng more than loud laughter.

great things labouring . . . birth Their ambitious projects fail before they properly begin.

A right description of our sport A very suitable description of our late efforts (to amuse the ladies).

Anointed An affected way of addressing an anointed sovereign.

utter a brace of words Make a brief introduction ('brace' is a pair).

a man of God's making Proverbial expression for someone who is at least human in appearance. In modern words, 'Can he be a Christian?'

my fair, sweet, honey monarch Armado is still addressing the King!

to *fortuna de la guerra* (Folio *delaguar*) to the fortunes of war (i.e. take a chance on Holofernes's performance). Omission of 'la' is typical of an Englishman quoting from Italian, while in the very next sentence 'the peace of mind' shows a foreigner's insistence on the article.

couplement Pair (an affected word). It may be presumed that the King and the Princess have now seated themselves in readiness for the performance.

Here is like to be i.e. we have the promise of. Reading from the paper handed him by Armado.

a good presence An impressive assembly.

You are deceived It is the King, who, in Costard's words, would scarcely get a living by 'reckoning'. This frequent by-play on numbers is lost on us.

hedge-priest Illiterate country parson. Berowne is using the least complimentary expressions.

Abate throw at novum Either (1) take away one throw, or (2) apart from a throw of nine. The dice game of 'Novum Quinque', for five players, was so-called from the winning throws, nine and five.

pick-out Select. From pricking a hole against a name or item in a list.

take each one in his vein Considering their various talents (ironic).

With libbard's head on knee i.e. a leopard's head represented at the knee joint in whatever armour Costard is wearing.

targe Another name for a shield.

before the legs A shocking pun on 'arms'.

I had done i.e. I would have done – said no more.

scutcheon Shield with coat-of-arms.

plain declares Clearly shows.

too right Alexander is said to have had a twist to the left (of his head).

most tender-smelling knight A reference to another peculiarity of the conqueror: his skin smelt sweetly.

Your servant, and Costard Obeying Berowne's summons, but in his own person.

overthrown i.e. disgraced (him) by your performance, but there is play on the idea of a conqueror being 'overthrown'.

painted cloth The Nine Worthies, with appropriate coats-of-arms, figured in contemporary wall-hangings. By 'you' Costard means the picture of Alexander.

Your lion . . . close-stool A facetious description of the arms of this Alexander: the heraldic lion holds a battle-axe (lengthened by Costard to a pole-axe) and another feature is dubbed a closet. The smuttiness is continued with a pun on Ajax and 'a jakes', a toilet.

bowler Player at bowls.

o'er-parted Cast above his capacity.

Cerberus The three-headed dog (in Latin *canis*), which guarded the entrance to the underworld.

shrimp Still used in some parts for a diminutive person: applicable, perhaps, to Moth, but hardly to the infant Hercules.

manus The word in Latin for either one hand or both.

Quoniam Since. A Latin word as superfluous to the conversation as *canis*, *manus* and *Ergo* (therefore).

Keep some state in thy exit Withdraw with dignity (difficult for an 'imp').

A Judas! A traitor! From Christ's false disciple, with whom the greatest of the 'Maccabees', who led the struggle for Jewish independence against the Syrians in the second century BC, was, and often is, confused.

clipt Cut short (i.e. without his surname of Maccabaeus, the 'Hammerer'). Pun on 'yclept' and followed with another pun with 'clip', an old word for 'embrace'. Judas would embrace Jesus in order to betray Him with a kiss.

To make Judas hang himself To bring the shame of suicide on himself by remorse afterwards.

elder Legend refers to a fig-tree. There is a pun on 'elder' (my better).

Because thou hast no face The far-fetched descriptions that follow are doubtless directed to the helmet worn by Holofernes over his face.

cittern-head The carved head of a kind of guitar.

head of a bodkin Elaborate heads of these pins, for use in the hair, were fashionable at this time.

death's face in a ring Also fashionable were rings with a skull and the words *memento mori*.

pommel of Caesar's falchion Knob at the end of the hilt (handle) of Caesar's sword (once a familiar museum 'exhibit').

Saint George's half-cheek The profile of the face of England's patron saint.

a brooch of lead i.e. a cheap one, used as a professional sign.

put thee in countenance i.e. given you a face.

outfaced them all Treated them all brazenly.

an ass i.e. disguised in a lion's skin.

adieu Probably a pun with Jew in Jude (a further 'clipping').

baited A word unfortunately often associated with Jews.

Achilles The great Greek antagonist of Hector, who was the son of Priam, King of Troy, and the leader of the Trojans.

come home by me Are returned on my own head.

but a Troyan in respect of this i.e. a mere Trojan warrior in comparison with the figure that has just emerged.

clean-timbered Well-built.

best indued in the small Most gifted in the part of the leg below the calf.

makes faces Pun on 'creating' faces and 'pulling' them. Armado's frustration is apparent.

armipotent Powerful in arms. A rare archaic epithet of Mars, the god of war, paraphrased in the second half of the line.

gilt nutmeg This aromatic seed of an oriental tree, then used to flavour ale or medicine (like the clove-stuck lemon), was also, when 'gilded' with egg-yolk, used as a seasonal (lover's) gift. Most inappropriate for a man of war.

cloven A pointless pun, hinting at the devil's presence.

Peace! Armado at last asserts himself.

the heir of Ilion The son of the Trojan King. In apposition to Hector.

breathed In such good condition.

out of his pavilion i.e. leaving his tent for the battle-field.

I am that flower He has no chance to complete this sentence.

rein thy tongue Control yourself.

against Hector i.e. in competition with a Hector who runs. A popular name for a hound.

The sweet war-man i.e. Hector. 'Sweet' is Armado's constant epithet.

forward with my device On with my speech.

bestow on me . . . hearing Not, as it would seem, 'enable me to hear', but 'give ear to me'.

surmounted Surprised.

The party is gone – This baffling line, italicized in the Folio (possibly a stage-direction), is given by some to Armado in his own person, by others to Costard. Where did Costard get his sudden piece of news? Some think Berowne, who has been silent for some time, must have slipped out and returned to inflame Costard.

Fellow Hector i.e. you scoundrel, Armado. In the build-up that follows the actors are still called in mockery by the names of their respective Worthies.

play the honest Troyan i.e. marry her. The word 'Trojan' (so applicable here) has long been used for 'good hard-working fellow'.

inflamonize Even in trouble Armado has to experiment with words.

potentates Princes.

for Pompey that is dead by him i.e. for the murder (in a duel) of himself, Costard.

great, great . . . Pompey Mocking Costard's threatening attitude to
  Armado.

Ates Ate, a daughter of Jupiter, was the Greek goddess of evil,
  especially in causing quarrels.

By the north pole An unusual oath, less to freeze his opponent with
  terror than to supply a pun.

like a northern man i.e. like a border raider with a long stave as his
  weapon.

bepray An unusual hybrid word, formed by association with the purely
  Saxon word 'beseech': 'I pray and beseech you . . .'

let me borrow my arms again As Pompey, he laid his arms at the feet
  of the Princess, possibly forgetting he would need them again as (?)
  Hannibal.

take you a buttonhole lower i.e. help you off with your coat, with the
  suggestion that he is going to 'take him down a peg' by exposing his
  lack of a shirt. Moth then protests that, as Costard is stripping for the
  fight, his master will lose face if he does not follow his example.

may and will i.e. may deny it and will do so.

woolward i.e. with the wool of the outer garment next to the skin,
  sometimes as a penance.

enjoined him Imposed on him as a penance.

in Rome i.e. when he was there on pilgrimage to obtain remission for
  his sins.

dishclout Cloth used by Jaquenetta when washing dishes.

for my life! An expression of horrified anticipation.

My tale is told i.e. you have spoken my message.

Worthies, away! The scene is no longer one of farce.

breathe free breath i.e. he has been suddenly released from an
  undignified quarrel.

I have seen . . . discretion To see daylight when it is visible only
  through a small hole was proverbial for being quick on the uptake.
  Armado expands the expression to refer to the wrong done by him to
  Jaquenetta and to the discreet action needed to put things right.

your Majesty Addressing her as if she were now sovereign on the
  death of her father.

The liberal opposition of our spirits The freedom with which we
  engaged in witty contests.

converse of breath Wordy exchanges. 'Converse' also meant
  'conversation' in the sixteenth century.

Your gentleness Was guilty of it i.e. your courtesy encouraged our
  impertinence.

bears not a humble tongue Is too upset to convey thanks in a suitably
  respectful manner.

my great suit The mission on which she had been sent to Navarre.

The extreme parts of time The artificiality of the King's speech is a foil
  to Berowne's 'honest plain words', which, however, can only be
  described as somewhat less elaborate than his sovereign's. The first

four lines may be paraphrased thus: In its final period time severely shapes all matters towards a swift determination of them and often, at the last critical moment (like the loosing of an arrow from a bow) brings the decisive result that protracted negotiations could not obtain.

the mourning brow of progeny i.e. the sad features of the French King's daughter.

Forbid the smiling courtesy . . . convince Deny to those paying court with (contrasting) smiles the promise of marriage, which they would gladly obtain by their argument.

justle it Divert it (by jostling).

to wail friends lost i.e. to mourn a dead father.

wholesome-profitable Good for the health. It is no wonder that this insensitive remark is incomprehensible to the Princess.

My griefs are double The emendations 'deaf' and 'dull' would wrongly suggest that the Princess's emotions prevent her from grasping what the King has said, whereas it is his whole utterance that lacks understanding. It is a delicate compliment to her host for her to describe her grief at her father's death as being 'doubled' by the necessity to quit Navarre.

badges i.e. the tokens given to the ladies.

deformed us Changed us for the worse (once the opposite of 'reformed').

the opposed end of our intents The opposite of what we intended (in our vows).

unbefitting strains Undignified tendencies.

wanton Frolicsome, undisciplined.

Formed by the eye Berowne's favourite theme of love kindled by looking into the eyes.

Which parti-coated presence . . . gravities i.e. if this clownish appearance of light love-making assumed by us has in your view suited ill with our solemn vows.

oaths and gravities Grave oaths (hendiadys).

that look into these faults That find out these faults in us.

Suggested us to make Tempted us to make (these mistakes).

the error that love makes i.e. our foolish behaviour is part of the love that now is yours.

By being once false . . . you i.e. by breaking our vows in order to pledge our truth to you.

both i.e. both false and true.

Thus purifies itself . . . grace i.e. (our oath-breaking) is purged (by the love that caused it) and becomes sacred.

rated Assessed their value.

bombast Cotton wool used as padding for clothes.

to the time i.e. to fill out the time.

in our respects In our regard for you.

quote them so Notice them as such.

dear Pun on (1) grievous, and (2) affectionate.

therefore this i.e. the penalty she imposes, explained in the rest of her speech.

as there is no such cause i.e. not that I should be regarded as causing you to fall in love with me.

naked hermitage Unfurnished or unoccupied hermit's hut.

celestial signs i.e. the Zodiac, whose twelve signs cover a year.

thin weeds Thin clothing.

But that it bear . . . love But let it endure this test and continue to be love. (Note that here 'love' repeats the final word of the previous line, and may, therefore, be a misprint).

these deserts These actions deserving reward.

intitled Written boldly.

To flatter up . . . rest i.e. to gratify my senses with idle comfort.

And what to me . . . sick These six lines anticipate, and are probably a first draft of, lines 838–55: 'Studies my lady . . .' Marked for deletion, it will have been printed all the same. As a rule Berowne's lines come last of the four suitors', as a climax.

A wife? Editors dispute whether this is an exclamation or a question, and whether spoken by Katharine or Dumain.'I thank you, gentle wife' supports Dumain.

three-fold i.e. three wishes with three times the usual love.

smooth-faced Pun on (1) too young for a beard, and (2) persuasive.

black gown i.e. Court mourning.

stay Wait.

The liker you The more like you ('long' in both time and Longaville).

Few taller are so young Few can be taller and yet so young.

What humble suit . . . there (See) what a lowly petition looks for a favourable reply from you there (in my eye).

the world's large tongue i.e. your reputation far and wide.

replete with mocks Brimming over with mockery of others.

estates Social ranks.

To weed this wormwood . . . brain To eradicate this bitterness from your fertile mind.

speechless sick . . . groaning wretches All in extremity: unable to converse and not in the mood to smile.

still converse Talk continually.

pained impotent Invalid suffering pain and incapable of smiling.

to choke a gibing spirit To stop the mouth of a mocker.

Whose influence . . . fools Whose effectiveness (as a joker) is fed by the uncritical applause accorded to clowns by hearers who will laugh at the feeblest jests (an immemorial practice).

A jest's prosperity . . . makes it A joke is successful when the audience laughs, not when it is uttered.

sickly ears The invalids listening to you.

hear your idle scorns i.e. pay attention to your mocking remarks.

have you and that fault withal i.e. take you, together with your tendency to mock.

Right joyful Referring to herself.

Ay, sweet my lord The Princess agrees with something the King has just said to her (aside).

Jack hath not Jill i.e. this is not a happy lovers' ending.

These ladies' courtesy . . . comedy i.e. had they accepted our suits now, there would have been the usual happy end to a *comedy*, after a plot in which the characters have been amusingly at odds with each other.

it wants It lacks only.

'twill end i.e. your 'comedy' will be over.

a votary One bound by a vow. A mocking echo of the first scene.

the dialogue This implies two opposing arguments, Spring v Winter, but the unfavourable aspects of the rival seasons are brought out in their respective and rather realistic lyrics.

the two learned men Holofernes and Nathaniel.

This side The singers are arranged in two groups.

the one maintained One side upheld.

pied Two-coloured. 'Daisies pied' and 'violets blue' are used by Milton in *L'Allegro* (lines 75 and 21).

lady-smocks Another name for the 'cuckoo-flower' (*Cardamine pratensis*).

cuckoo-buds Unidentified, possibly buttercups or bird's foot trefoil.

oaten straws Lengths of oat straw cut into pipes.

ploughmen's clocks To get them up early in the morning.

turtles tread Turtle-doves mate.

blows his nail i.e. blows on his fingers to warm them.

ways be foul Roads are muddy.

keel Cool (the contents) by stirring. A dialect variant of 'cool'.

coughing drowns the parson's saw i.e. the coughing of the congregation renders the parson's wise sayings inaudible.

roasted crabs Wild apples roasted and put into bowls of ale.

The words of Mercury i.e. the prose he now speaks to direct the two sides off the stage, or to part actors and audience. Mercury was the eloquent messenger of the gods, as Apollo was their musician.

Revision questions on Act V

1 To what extent did the two sets of entertainers fail in their efforts?

2 Give an account of the parts played in this Act by (a) Boyet and (b) Moth.

3 The action of the play begins and ends with a message from France. Show how each has contributed to the wording of the title *Love's Labour's Lost*.

4 Describe three different ways in which wrong done is 'righted'.

Shakespeare's art in *Love's Labour's Lost*

Thou art not for an age but for all time (Ben Jonson).

Introduction

Shakespeare achieved two 'firsts' in our national literature, as poet and as playwright – something not claimed for any man of letters in any other nation. His plays have received worldwide recognition; his poetry is embedded in the dialogue of those plays. His powers of expression matched his genius in the creation of character. His lines, the best of which are poetically inspired, were composed for the utterance of professional actors entertaining audiences of varying tastes. He knew his fellow-actors and the roles they were best at undertaking. Through them as mouthpieces he was also at work on the minds of those who watched his dramas unfold, showing them human nature at its best and at its worst, stimulating their imagination by bringing old stories to life before their eyes and affording them opportunities to exercise their judgement between right and wrong, loyalty and treachery, love and hate, wisdom and folly. The audience beheld good and evil deeds, understood the motives and flinched at the consequences. All the world became a stage presenting in turn sad and comic aspects of the life they themselves were living; they learned to laugh at themselves and, perhaps, even to change their ways.

For generations it has been argued that Shakespeare's marvellous inventions could not possibly be the work of a countryman come up to town; the mystery of his personality, on the other hand, reinforces the appeal of his creations. He was many sided, with no bias, no doctrine to preach, no malice towards his contemporaries, no subservience to authority and no respect for mobs; he sculpted life, from the beautiful to the grotesque, without sentiment or cynicism. What personal feelings he had – attractions to friends and emotional involvements with women – he expressed in a few poems and sonnets that cannot be positively said to be either based on real experience or written merely as literary exercises. In brief, Shakespeare was a poetical dramatist, not a poet who used the forms of drama, as did on occasion our second greatest poet, John Milton. It is the poetry that enriches the study of his work away from the stage and endows his characters with the immortality of endless editions.

Shakespeare's greatness was acknowledged in his own day, and his works, while they fluctuated in public esteem during the following centuries, have never been more popular than during the past hundred years. Scholars in various parts of the world have devoted years, in some cases a lifetime, to wider and more intensive research into the texts, and to the discovery of fresh clues and new interpretations. In all but a few of his plays his imagination and wealth of diction have stirred the hearts of full houses – the voices may change, but the words are the same. The Old Vic took five years to present the entire series; a similar enterprise on the television screen has been undertaken by the BBC. None of his plays was written for the study: all had to come across the boards to that sea of faces on whose reception (handclaps or hisses) depended their success or failure. Least of all would their author have expected to be a staple topic for generations of students taking English Literature.

In the following commentary opinions are those arrived at or accepted by the editor; they are offered to the student as an aid to forming his own judgements and, it is hoped, to getting more enjoyment from the play. There is little in this, Shakespeare's earliest comedy, that is not, to our tastes, extremely artificial: much of the dialogue is strained and there seems too much of it at times; incidents are few and mostly absurd in some degree; the human relationships lack depth of feeling, despite extravagant phraseology.

We may ask what was Shakespeare's purpose – unless, as some do, we prefer to dismiss the whole production as a failure in apprenticeship. We notice much topical material slipped in everywhere: was this a natural desire to succeed with a sophisticated audience? And is it largely lost on us who belong to a very different generation? Does the student, after seeing the play recently performed on both stage and TV screen or imagining it for himself, honestly find it amusing, if only in patches? Or should he content himself with evaluating it as a satirical social study mocking contemporary fashions and witty exchanges? Does he support earlier suggestions by some scholars that this is Shakespeare at his worst, or even not Shakespeare at all? Or does he detect the dramatist's own hand in these attempts at character-contrast, these wild verbal encounters, these embarrassing revelations – in fact, a first blend of those devices that became more convincing and more opposite in the mature comedies? Underneath the often crude mockery is there more than a touch of the man who knew so well his London and his Stratford?

Structure

The student will find great interest in contrasting this, the first of his plays, with *The Tempest*, generally regarded as his last, and in considering the development in dramatic construction, human characterization and poetic imagination that took place between 1593 and 1613. What the two have in common is something structurally unusual in Shakespeare: a certain unity of place – here the various parts of the park of a great house, there different points on a small island somewhere in the Mediterranean. Both have the strongest distinctions between the cultured and the boorish, between the main and the subordinate plot. They differ in their ends: in the early play the transgressors are suitably punished, in the later all are forgiven.

Division into acts and scenes in the Folios and the Quartos is irregular; in our play there are no numbered scenes and the fifth act is misprinted 'Actus Quartus'. The second scene of this act is inordinately long, the longest in Shakespeare, whereas Act III is exceptionally short. In fact we have really a succession of scenes, marked off by exits and entrances, alternately from the main and the sub-plot, but with intrusions into the one by characters from the other – that mingling of two strands of action in which Shakespeare was to excel. It is Armado, guest of Navarre's court, who, by observing Costard with his wench and coveting her, links the two plots together, while Costard's confusing of the letters leads to a sudden change of fortune. Shakespeare's plots not only interweave two or more distinct stories, but rely for further effect on doubling: besides two letters (which are contrasted) the exchange of the letters is paralleled by the exchange of tokens; there are two attempts to entertain, both consisting of disguises (live Russians and dead Worthies); and there are two cases of overhearing, one seen by the audience, the other reported.

The first editions of the plays were as innocent of location and lists of characters as the boards themselves were, as we have seen, bare of stage-settings. Later editors supplied the names of towns, streets, apartments and fields. In *Love's Labour's Lost* they could do no better than 'The King of Navarre's park' for the first scene, and 'The same' for all the rest. Of local features or time of day there is next to no indication: Boyet's sycamore in some other part of the park, or the King's invitation to a dance on the 'grass'. How much richer in its appeal to the senses is Prospero's isle!

This is indeed less a play of action than of dialogue. The audience has to follow not so much the change of emotions or the revelation of character as the play on words, the swift interchange of figurative terms and classical allusions, and the sometimes extreme burlesques of lover, courtier and scholar. The action which gives rise to so much strained and artificial, and often fantastic and irrational dialogue, is caused entirely by chance. Chance brings a bevy of charming ladies on the scene when the ink is scarcely dry on the signatures of the devotees who have forsworn the company of all women; by mere chance Berowne encounters Costard and decides to entrust his love-missive to him; death with customary unexpectedness brings the farce to a sober conclusion, just at the moment when the chastened lovers are salving their consciences in uproarious mirth at the expense of two quarrelling 'Worthies'.

Setting

In spite of the play's foreign setting, we really find ourselves looking on at happenings in some English nobleman's country seat, where the guests give a native rendering of the extravagant wit, the literary affectation and the character-assassination, then the sport of this generation on the Continent. For the King of Navarre's park we could well read Windsor Forest. Here are dull-witted constables, pedantic schoolmasters, dairymaids with roving eyes and cheeky boys, a world in which, even up at the great house, elaborate gestures are seen as an intrusion from 'abroad', to be mimicked from behind.

While we see nothing of the pavilions to which the visitors retire, or the deer they are intended to shoot, the reality of this English landscape is impressed upon us by those passing allusions to country life and customs which are a vital part of Shakespeare's genius. Amid the torrent of shocking puns and earthy innuendoes we are of an England now known as the 'Elizabethan Age', built up from scattered details: games of bowls, dice and backgammon; dances from the stately 'measure' to the grotesque 'antic', knot gardens and more spacious beds where damask roses blow and lilies unfold; dim lights from tapers and the excitement of 'fire-works'; sacks brought to the mill and fairings brought home from fairs; malmsey wine to drink and tasty morsels like gingerbread and flapdragons. Then there was the periodical bleeding and the unseasonable visits of the plague, like late frosts in Spring; bird-bolts and the arrows from cross-bows in the covert; law-officers like 'apparitors' and law terms like 'quillets'; the dark hints of secrets extorted on the 'rack'; the novelty of Negroes with their swarthy skins and Russians in their furs; the fashionable superiority of blondes over brunettes; tented fields and riders in the lists; the mockery of 'cuckolds' whose wives have been unfaithful. Also, the much-worn 'hornbook' from which the young child learns his alphabet; the despised occupation of 'reckoning', especially when practised by a 'tapster'.

There was that other numbering, in metre, employed by the lover and the poet to express emotions, in ballad and sonnet; and from end to end that bold experimentation with words which was the besetting pursuit of that adventurous age. Many hundreds of extraordinary vocables were to perish as soon as they were coined; many more changed in pronunciation and meaning in the following centuries – hence the need for editors! One scholar has made a list of over two hundred words in *this* play which occur nowhere else in Shakespeare. So many out-of-date expressions are to a modern audience tokens of a time as remote and romantic as the country of Navarre was to the author's contemporaries in pit and balcony. The classical allusions typical of an early Shakespeare play and not entirely lost on the pit, quite apart from the balcony, when fresh from his quill, have had to be carefully explained in the textual notes.

The characters

Of the various categories of Shakespeare's characters represented in different plays, three appear in this one: mannered courtiers, pedantic scholars and self-confident rustic officials. Here we are given first sketches, in which peculiarities are exaggerated sometimes beyond the bounds of the ridicule that amuses. All three kinds, however, get appropriate treatment without any stress on class distinctions: Shakespeare's dramatic contrasts are based not on status, but on human qualities. Already in *Love's Labour's Lost* we see the familiarity with which characters from widely varying social spheres meet and mix, just as his plots skilfully blend tragic and comic. Even Holofernes (V,2,623) and Costard (IV,3,209) achieve a measure of dignity. The arrogant are discomfited, not because of who they are but what they are. Whitehall and Stratford compete on fairly equal terms.

There is of course the contrast that extends through all literature – that between the sexes – in which personal attraction is balanced against sharp contests of wit. In Shakespeare's comedies the women seem to hold the upper hand; none of his other men are as loquacious as Berowne, but even he meets his match in Rosaline. Those champions of women who resent the role of Petruchio in *The Taming of the Shrew* and therefore the play as a whole, not only fail to appreciate its final scene but do not recognize Shakespeare's assessment, which was largely a contemporary one: men give the orders, women inspire devotion. Liberty and equality were abstractions in an age that set more value on order and obedience. The King of Navarre issued what amounted to an order to his obedient Court; the Princess and her ladies inspired its cancellation (or at least a reduction to one-third of the term). One interesting contrast between the sexes in the play is that the men hide their secrets from one another; the women share theirs with much banter. Another contrast is drawn (topically) between the rival blondes and brunettes: the heroine is a brunette in a world where blonde hair is the fashion, and her colour gets much unfavourable comment.

Royalty

There is an air of artificiality about the two Courts, the resident one and the visitors'. They are evenly balanced, their affections symmetrically distributed, their movements largely in unison, and their speech almost exchangeable (in fact some lines have, in print, found their way into the wrong mouths – or have they?). The comic characters, however exaggerated their mannerisms, move about in the light of common day; the courtiers inhabit a world of their own, in which from start to finish each is absorbed by thoughts of the lady he has already once met, the passing fancy for whom swiftly develops into the passion which indites poems. If absence makes the heart grow fonder, then the King's strange whim, in keeping a distance between women and students, is the powerful factor in four simultaneous likings leading to four certain, if delayed, marriages.

The King's overriding ambition may have been to acquire for his small kingdom (or the intellectual part of it) a reputation for a scholarship of truly Renaissance proportions; however, the Renaissance was, as never before, alive to the power of the senses. Whether Navarre had any conception of the impossible commitment he was imposing on his followers can only be guessed at; royal orders and counter-orders were not to be judged by their consistency in the heyday of Tudor monarchy. He is a likeable sovereign (as the real Henry of Navarre was popular with most of his subjects) and shows both dignity and tolerance, especially of the thrustful Berowne, whose eloquence and reasoning easily outshine his own rather stilted speeches.

Addressed as 'my lord' or 'my liege' by his courtiers, the King is plain 'Navarre' to Boyet, who has a contemporary French noble's patronizing attitude to a minor kingdom. On stage he conveys the impression of some English duke at home in his own country, whose physical appearance is unknown (in days when anonymity remained undisturbed by the press photographer) to the local constable, when he insists on speaking to 'the duke's own person'. Even Armado, while talking of 'the King', cannot but echo the mode of address in this country to which he is a visitor and refer to 'his Grace'. Somehow a 'King' at large in the English provinces must have seemed strange where a Queen had ruled so long.

His instant regard for the Princess, marked and enlarged on

by Boyet, in whom, as her attendant lord, perhaps there may have lurked a spark of jealousy, leads him to a generous reaction to the grasping request of the old French monarch. Nevertheless, loyal to his oath, he decides not to receive the ladies within the gates. This distinction, between the Court and the park, seems a dishonest compromise forced upon the King by diplomatic considerations (and was the distance between the two a good English mile?). When the King weakens so far as to suggest dispensing with the decree against speaking with a woman, on the excuse of 'necessity', Berowne signs with a flourish and boasts that he will be the last to break his word. After Navarre has welcomed the ladies to their tents and left for the Court, his three followers in turn leave him to steal back for a further look. His 'sentence' at the end of the play to twelve months in a solitary hermitage seems less severe when we consider that his idea of imposing three years of a monastic existence on three young men was nothing short of tyrannical.

The anonymous Princess has caused much guessing about her possible identity in continental affairs. Whatever her actual age, we have the impression of youth, culture and a discreet firmness. She consciously hands over to Rosaline, just as the King is, on occasion, content for Berowne to assume the leadership. She controls her ladies and in argument is more than a match for Navarre. She shows spirit in her first reaction to her unconventional reception and in her exchanges with Boyet; she obviously prefers the honesty of the forester to the flattery of the courtier. She is mischievously quick to suggest the exchange of favours and is supremely dignified under the shock of her father's death. Two touches endear her to an audience: her feeling for the deer to be shot at and her readiness to encourage local talent, however feeble its nature. Where Navarre sought to impose three years' abstinence for no valid reason, she finds in the Court mourning justifiable occasion to make such abstinence a reality for the time being.

The leading couple

The heroines of Shakespeare's major comedies – Beatrice, Portia, Rosalind, Viola – by sheer charm and force of personality rise superior to their male partners. This quality is foreshadowed in the earlier comedies, even in Katharina the Shrew, whose concluding speech is marked by serenity and self-control, and whose character has been changed by her taming; less wild, though equally spirited, our Rosaline emerges not victorious, but exercising judgement in words similarly apt and well chosen, while revealing that she has made her choice. She is the one lady in attendance capable of taking the Princess's place; she strikes a bolder note and mercilessly teases the King. She might well be modelled on the *Dark Lady of the Sonnets*, her locks of ebony being strenuously defended against the fair ones both by Berowne and by herself.

Thus she is fitted to confront Berowne, whose long speeches – wordy protests, voluble soliloquies, philosophic harangues and caustic portraits – dominate the play. It must be admitted that in neither of them is there great depth or development of charac- ter: all is incident and backchat. Berowne the mocker chastises others with verbal whips: the forsworn, the blunderer, the post- urer, the spoilsport, the affected speaker. Most of all he lashes himself (though not in public!). Less brutal than Petruchio, more determined than Benedick, he uses words as his weapons; his monologues savour more of a delight in hearing himself speak than a desire to communicate emotion.

Berowne has much sage advice to give: he warns against the stupefying effect of excessive study, the neglect of the inspir- ation that comes naturally from feminine eyes, the vanity of dressing up, whether in fancy clothes or high-flown figures of speech. He scorns impracticable schemes and conventional artificiality, both features of Elizabethan society. In his sincere moments he prefers plain words: 'My love to thee is sound', yet even here he is self-decoyed into a piece of the very ostentation he has just condemned: '*sans* crack or flaw'. He is quick to recognize the change from comedy to tragedy and dismisses the 'Worthies'. His turn has always come as a climax (unless his betrayal by his own letter is really an anti-climax); so does his punishment – to exercise his genius as a comic on those who can only groan.

The Spanish knight

An English audience, familiar for decades with Spanish embass- ies and recently cock-a-hoop over the destruction of the 'magni- ficent' Armada, would enjoy this burlesque of the proud,

mannered Spaniard. We hear his elaborate sentences, the cumu-
lative titles and heaped-up epithets, and the roll-call of synonyms before he appears on the stage in person, in the letter
reporting his handing over of Costard to the constable, while
taking the offending female into his personal custody.

Don Adriano de Armado, as he signs himself, is constantly
accompanied by a diminutive page with a name more suited to
one of the fairies in *A Midsummer Night's Dream*. Armado is
melancholy because he is in love and asks Moth for examples of
great men in a similar state of mind; because he is ashamed of
having been fascinated by a dairymaid, he prefers the case of
King Cophetua and the beggar maid. He then embarks on an
odd intrigue, releasing Costard to carry another extraordinary
epistle, this time to the dairymaid (as *his* beggar maid), who also
happens to be a woman with whom he accused the bearer of his
letter of associating!

Also puzzling is the fact that, despite his exaggerated air of
confidence, he seeks ideas from others: he catechizes Moth,
partly for information, partly to see what this quick-witted sprig
will say next. Asked by the King to provide entertainment, he
seeks out the schoolmaster for suggestions. In fact, he is a
windbag with an extensive vocabulary, some of which he has
freshly coined, who cuts a disappointing figure after the King's
effusive commendation; the few and feeble lines uttered by
'Hector' in a would-be epic tone of voice are the only hint of
what Navarre promised from him: romances of knights-errant
of dusky Spain. Even in soliloquy, with himself as his only
audience, he pursues vain figures of speech and classical
allusions; since he is in love he must, like all fashionable lovers,
'turn sonnet'. But his utterances rarely stray into metre; the six
lines, forming a sextet or concluding part of a sonnet, at the end
of his letter to Jaquenetta seem utterly incongruous – did he
copy them from lines left lying about by some poetaster in the
neighbourhood? The transition from kissing her foot to
threatening to devour her is as abrupt as the change from prose
to verse.

It is as impossible for Armado to rhyme as it is for him to
perpetrate a pun; his rhetoric is the fantastic or 'new-minted'
expression, his logic the answering of his own questions. He is
the prose counterpart of the rhythmical Berowne. Berowne's
punishment is romantic marriage deferred, Armado's is prosaic

marriage as in duty bound. He apologizes for the harshness of the few prose words of farewell after the singing has stopped; the last allusion of this loquacious bird-of-passage through the Court of Navarre is to Mercury – the god of travellers and of eloquence!

Two learned men

Not until Act IV do those leading intellects of the English village, *the parson* and *the schoolmaster*, put in an appearance. Their part in the action is, first, to receive the second mis-directed letter and send it on again to the last person its writer would have liked it to go; and, second, to fill out the cast of the Nine Worthies. Unlike the corresponding characters immortalized by Oliver Goldsmith in *The Deserted Village*, these two are, along with Armado, caricatures; yet, however ridiculous their literary jargon – peppered with Latin tags – they are more human, more appealing to an English audience than the lords and ladies, whose over-refined persiflage belongs to the rarefied atmosphere of a remote Court. When we listen to these two, accompanied by the inarticulate constable, we are in the grounds of the nearest manor house.

Holofernes, also called the 'Pedant' (i.e. a schoolmaster, and not, as today, one who parades his knowledge), dominates his companions as Berowne does his. He would also seem to have a professional reputation, since Armado has heard of him, and a parent of one of his pupils has invited him to dinner. In his presentation of Judas Maccabaeus he makes a bolder stand than the others against the ragging. Ardent research has failed to provide any proof that he is a burlesque of some schoolmaster of Shakespeare's young days.

When Jaquenetta enters, however, it is to the gentler and less formidable Nathaniel, the Curate, that she applies. This 'foolish, mild man' is miscast as the conquering Alexander: the 'world's commander' is more at home on a bowling-green.

Costard the clown

The word 'clown' for a paid jester (also 'fool' in Shakespeare) is derived from the boorish or comic behaviour of the simple peasant or 'clown'. It is as the latter that Costard is almost invariably referred to in the stage directions; in only two of these, as well as in Jaquenetta's words and Moth's pun on the large round apple called a 'costard', do we find his real name. In the presence of the others, all of whom can read and write, he would seem a typical ignorant rustic, easily imposed on by those whose language is above his head: arrested by Armado (on dubious authority) for meeting Jaquenetta; condemned by the King (who is about to offend against his own regulation); sent away to prison in the custody of the page after having to witness Armado's shameless attempt to obtain an assignation from Jaquenetta; then released by the knight to carry his love-letter to the girl – and being paid stingily for doing so!

At this point Costard surreptitiously takes control of events by a trick which seems innocent enough on the part of an illiterate peasant and even devoid of malice to a watchful audience. Entrusted by Berowne (who got to know him while transferring him to the care of Armado) with a second letter to a lady at the Court, he exchanges them. First he takes Armado's to the Princess for delivery to Rosaline, which results in some embarrassment and some teasing by Boyet. Here Costard, whose zest for fine words has been sharpened by his contact with courtly conversation, joins in the verbal contests and even, when left to himself, boasts of having played his part in humiliating Boyet – 'a most simple clown', he calls him.

Costard puts Jaquenetta forward as the recipient of Berowne's letter and, when Holofernes sends her off with it to the King, he gleefully escorts her thither. Because he has been told that it might 'concern much', Costard chooses (not unnaturally for the period in which he lives) to suggest to the King that treason is involved. The man he thus betrays, whether consciously or not, uses on him the strongest language in the play. Undeterred, he turns to embrace his Jaquenetta and, when dismissed from the scene as an undesirable witness of the general embarrassment, utters with refreshing native cunning one of the most pregnant lines in the play: 'Walk aside the true folk [i.e. the honest lovers], and let the traitors [i.e. the oath-breakers or the authors of the mysterious "treason"] stay.'

The honest but muddle-headed Costard says some contradictory things in a convincing manner, though he anticipates Mrs Malaprop frequently. His kindly nature would accept Moth, even as a bastard son, for being cheeky to Holofernes; after upbraiding Nathaniel for letting the side down, he excuses him as a neighbourly soul. His own appearance as Pompey the 'Big' – compared by the King to a ship under full sail – was, in his own view, marred by only one little fault.

Moth

Whether his name is that of an insect or of a speck of dust (the 'mote' in IV,3,158 is spelt 'moth' in the Folio), this small boy with taking ways is no respecter of persons. Quick-witted and very ready with puns, he saves his rudest remarks for his asides. Yet, after sniping his way through the play, when he is himself sniped at – as he essays to deliver the script he has been given to learn – he pouts and scampers off the stage. Returning later as the infant Hercules he proves, before the 'presence majestical', to be not merely diminutive, but dumb. Moth is very probably a burlesque of the boy actors who performed plays by Lyly and were popular at Elizabeth's Court.

Boyet

As if one posturing foreigner were not enough, the Princess's usher and counsellor, Boyet, given a full-length caricature by Berowne in V,2,316–35, is another of a different kind. At one time he is offering state advice to his mistress, at another indulging in a frivolous tit-for-tat with her ladies. His chief part is to overhear the lords planning their disguise as Russians and give sufficient warning for a suitable reception; his account of what he saw is possibly as exaggerated as his gestures when engaged in formal ushering. He takes a full share in baiting the Worthies, with the result that Berowne forgives him for spoiling their sport and welcomes him as a fellow-mocker.

Style

The vocabulary of Shakespeare's works has been calculated to exceed fifteen thousand words, well ahead of his nearest competitor John Milton with eight thousand. They include many which, once in everyday Elizabethan use, are now obsolete, e.g. 'behests' (commands), others whose meanings have changed, e.g. 'harbour' (shelter, accommodation), or some which, already obsolete in conversation (archaisms) were used for poetic effect, e.g. 'eyne' (eyes). Shakespeare must have been an omnivorous reader, with a comprehensive memory. Such a well-stocked mind, combined with great imaginative powers, enabled him not only to compose the dialogue of lifelike characters, but also create the background and atmosphere in which they moved; whole passages have the substance of short poems, studded with literary allusions and topical references.

His earlier manner was often daringly experimental, trying out far-fetched analogies and intricate figures of speech; his 'middle period' as it has been called, struck a more even balance between idea and expression; in his great tragedies powerful emotions and a wealth of imagery break the restraints of precise grammar, plain logic and metrical regularity to reach an eloquence beyond what had gone before and rarely equalled since.

Love's Labour's Lost is an extreme example of the early manner. *Euphuism* (see Literary Terms), which seems to have appealed to the Queen herself, is resorted to in a play performed before her in her old age, a few years after its original composition, but it is carried to such lengths, both in the romantic main plot and in the comic sub-plot, that the prevailing impression is of satire – the dialogue is as unreal as the story. The trouble was that such an affected mode of expression could only be ridiculed in much that now seems tedious nonsense. The play seems to offer ample scope for clowning of different kinds, but it is not easy to make Armado or Boyet or Holofernes or Nathaniel really funny to a modern audience: we laugh more at their gestures than at their words – the appeal is less in what they say than in how they say it. In studying the text we realize there is excess in everything, and excess is one vehicle of satire.

Since Shakespeare seems to be mainly engaged in making fun of the extravagant fantasies of courtly love, or ostentatious displays of un-English behaviour, or the pedantic parade of pedagogic learning, there is little scope for serious comment on style. The audience is entertained to a steady stream of would-be witty puns on the one hand and uncouth errors on the other. Meanings are hidden in subtle phrases or lost in fanciful comparisons; words are played with like tennis-balls:

Well bandied both! A set of wit well played. (V,2,29)

The extent of the influence on the early Shakespeare of John Lyly (1553–1606) has been much debated. He was a university man, accepted at Elizabeth's court, where he became familiar with the sort of word-play he was to employ in his two 'novels' of *Euphues*. He wrote plays performed before the Queen by boys of the Chapel Royal and St Paul's (notice how the irrepressible Moth is easily put out before royalty). Into these were introduced lyrics, no doubt to give the boys a chance to use their singing voices (a practice, distinctive of Shakespeare's plays, which probably justifies the somewhat irrelevant verses to the Owl and the Cuckoo).

Don Adriano de Armado, by virtue of his appearing so often, plays a leading part in the parody of Euphuism. Examples of his linguistic excesses are the lavish forms of address: 'tender juvenal' and 'sweet smoke of rhetoric' (Moth), 'the welkin's vice-regent' (the King), 'men of peace' (the civilians, parson and schoolmaster). He personifies objects, as if they were extensions of himself: 'rust, rapier', 'write, pen'. It is very appropriate that we *hear* him before we see him, in the fantastic report read out by the King: in this and elsewhere we are offered, presumably in the interests of accuracy, synonyms in series, usually four: 'thou viewest, beholdest, surveyest or seest'. The simplest comes at the end like an anti-climax! Or the most ordinary name is introduced with a patronising flourish: 'nourishment which is called supper' (I,1,233), 'which the rude multitude call the afternoon' (V,1,81). The latter is glossed by Armado as 'the posteriors of this day', which grotesque phrase is commended by Holofernes, his friendly rival in concoction of verbiage, as 'well culled, chose, sweet and apt'.

While the fine-spun 'conceits' of the lords and ladies may be Shakespeare's travesty of the contemporary euphistic craze for saying something striking, the village worthies mouthing their 'scraps' from the 'feast of languages' are his own invention. The play is more liberally sprinkled than any other by Shakespeare with linguistic tags, Latin, French and even Italian; for this phenomenon the schoolmaster (technically the 'Pedant') is mainly responsible. This vain pedagogue, mercifully limited to the second half of the play, displays a familiarity with Latin syntax that Shakespeare may have owed to his schooldays in Stratford-upon-Avon. In Armado he meets a kindred spirit, though each has a frank opinion of the other: 'his general behaviour vain, ridiculous, and thrasonical' says Holofernes of the Spanish knight, while the latter warns the King that 'the schoolmaster is exceedingly fantastic; too, too vain.' The parson admiringly adds to his vocabulary, Dull and Costard make rustic mistakes, and Moth, in some ways the sanest member of the cast, puns aloud and aside, at the expense of the adults – a boy Cupid in the flesh! If the play *has* a theme, it might well be the hollowness of affectation, whether in behaviour or expression.

Verse and prose

Shakespeare's blank verse, rhymed and unrhymed, was used for passionate or poetical speeches, especially by the main characters; prose served for argument, cross-talk and documents, and particularly the speech of the lower ranks of society. In *Love's Labour's Lost* the abundance of rhyming lines (about half, greater than in any other play by Shakespeare, and a mark of early composition) has repeatedly influenced the choice of a word, often resulting in something unexpected or pointless. The rhymes come mostly in couplets, but there are frequent quatrains. These aids to artificial expression are far apart from the sonnets and lyrics that grace this play. Three of the lovers' poems appeared in 1599 in a pirated collection published by Wm Jaggard, *The Passionate Pilgrim By W. Shakespeare*. Nos. 3 and 5 are the fourteen-line sonnets of Longaville and Berowne; No. 18 is the trochaic octosyllabic piece of Dumain, which could then be styled a 'sonnet', as could also that of the King, which has sixteen lines and has not survived elsewhere. The songs of Spring and Winter achieved early fame on their own account and have found their way into various anthologies. In them Shakespeare's Warwickshire countryside was given full-throated utterance: the Owl was a native, the Cuckoo a foreigner.

Key-words

A lover's eyes will gaze an eagle blind;
A lover's ear will hear the lowest sound (IV,3,330–31).

These two lines from Berowne's hyperbole-ridden speech are representative of the part played by these two senses in this and other plays of Shakespeare. The eye, with its sight, its beams and its tears, receives much poetic treatment, often extravagant. Less frequently mentioned, the ear is active in eavesdropping, listening, acquiring new words, detecting errors and moving to music. Consciously or unconsciously, Shakespeare uses key-words in his drama to bring out contrasts or create atmosphere: in our play 'fair' and 'black', 'light' and 'dark' are frequently compared, favourably for one, unfavourably for the other; triple repetitions, e.g. 'sport' and 'power' are plentiful. So are threes of various kinds, topped by the mystical multiple, nine, though the art of reckoning may be deemed a menial occupation, fit only for a tapster!

L'envoy

Did William Shakespeare hugely enjoy himself indulging in these verbal fantasies (ingenious for the gallery, smutty for the pit), or was he, perhaps, conscious of falling short, with a resolve to do better next time? He must have laughed at his first band of comic characters; imperfect caricatures as they may appear to us (especially in the 'light' of his later achievements), there is an absence of cruelty in his satire, a presence of something sympathetic in the act of creating them, together with that love of language for its own sake which leads to poetic invention. Many of the thousand Shakespearian lines that Ben Jonson would have 'blotted' may be found in *Love's Labour's Lost,* but its author was still a young man, revelling in the give-and-take of anteroom and tavern; *his* marriage, too, had been hastened rather than delayed.

General questions

1 Illustrate, with particular reference to people and things, Berowne's habit of mockery.

Notes for use in answering this question:

Begin with Rosaline's judgement of him in Act V: 'a man replete with mocks' – so she had heard on all hands – no one escaped his wit – his method to make hurtful comparisons – his purpose to raise a laugh – he needed curing of this defect – the remedy: twelve months spent *daily* with sufferers in extreme agony, trying to raise a laugh; the test of a joke being the reaction of those listening to it.

Characteristic nevertheless of Berowne: 'befall what will befall, I'll jest a twelvemonth in a hospital' – cf. when King weakens, Berowne holds him to his resolve (Act I) – 'mere necessity'. Scoffs (not without some justification) at mere book-knowledge of stars – going blind poring over books instead of gaining 'light' from women's eyes – folly of studying 'out of season' (like snow in May).

After Armado's letter his remark 'best I ever heard' shows his earlier admiration was really mockery. After despatching Costard with the letter he mocks *himself* – the former love's whip is now enlisted in the service of Cupid. He is actually looking for a wife: a most erratic instrument needing constant attention – he had of course to choose the most sexy of the ladies – as punishment for his previous neglect of the love god his sighing, groaning, even writing poetry: he is the fool who sent the sonnet by a clown to the adored. When he finds he is not alone in love, mockery returns, and he has a rich field – he with the King and Longaville form a triangular gallows: symbol of the love that settles the fate of fools.

With Dumain as fourth victim he draws comparisons: another sack of grain to be ground – four game-birds roasted together. When he addresses the King his mockery strikes a more respectful note, but shows he has overheard the royal poem.

Rashly 'flouting' the other three he boasts his own constancy, abstaining from emotional outbursts which are so extreme that the King himself resembles a gnat caught in a sunbeam – now uses hyperboles in defence of the common lovesick state – in the masking he pleads, 'Vouchsafe to show the sunshine of your face!' Then he finds a new target in Boyet and his gestures: 'See where it comes' – but there is no mockery facing Rosaline: 'I am yours and all that I possess' – a last fling when he refers to the 'plague' afflicting all the men.

His own self-mockery finds further expression when, the King fearing disgrace from the performance of the Worthies, Berowne declares 'We are shame-proof, my lord' – he mocks Costard's wrath with 'Pompey the huge' – but he has the sense after the news of the French King's death to dismiss the Worthies with a remark from which all mockery has been banished: 'The scene begins to cloud'. (Was he Shakespeare himself, who tempered his mockery with humanity?)

2 Write an account of events as seen by Costard.
3 Which two incidents did you find most amusing? Why?
4 Write a critical appreciation of the last scene.
5 Which character provides the actor of it with the greatest challenge in interpretation?
6 What peculiarities of character and what redeeming qualities do you find in (a) Holofernes and (b) Armado?
7 How would you set the stage and arrange the movements for Act IV, Scene 3?
8 Do you consider Berowne to be a true lover? Are there any contradictions in his ideas and attitudes?
9 Write a short account of three verbal contests of different kinds.
10 How many written documents can you count? What does each contribute to the action?
11 Which in your opinion are the three best puns in the play? In what way are they effective?
12 What indications, apart from diction and costume, are there that the action does not take place in the twentieth century? Would you produce the play in a modern setting?
13 Besides iambic pentameter, how many kinds of verse are used in the play? Comment on the rhymed dialogue.
14 'There is too much symmetry and too little sympathy in *Love's Labour's Lost*.' Discuss.

Further reading

The Arden Shakespeare: Love's Labour's Lost ed. R. W. David (Methuen repr. 1980)

William Shakespeare, E. K. Chambers (Clarendon Press 1930)

Shakespeare, Sir Walter Releigh (Macmillan 1907)

Shakespeare and his World, F. E. Halliday (Thames & Hudson 1956)

Life in Shakespeare's England, J. D. Wilson (Macmillan 1913)

Everyman's Companion to Shakespeare, G. & B. Lloyd Evans (Dent 1978)

A Shakespeare Encyclopaedia, O. J. Campbell & E. G. Quinn (Methuen 1966)

A First Folio in reduced facsimile is probably available in a central reference library.

Pan study aids Titles published in the Brodie's Notes series

W. H. Auden Selected Poetry

Jane Austen Emma Mansfield Park Northanger Abbey Persuasion
Pride and Prejudice

Anthologies of Poetry Ten Twentieth Century Poets The Poet's Tale
The Metaphysical Poets

Samuel Beckett Waiting for Godot

Arnold Bennett The Old Wives' Tale

William Blake Songs of Innocence and Experience

Robert Bolt A Man for All Seasons

Harold Brighouse Hobson's Choice

Charlotte Brontë Jane Eyre

Emily Brontë Wuthering Heights

Robert Browning Selected Poetry

John Bunyan The Pilgrim's Progress

Geoffrey Chaucer (parallel texts editions) The Franklin's Tale
The Knight's Tale The Miller's Tale The Nun's Priest's Tale
The Pardoner's Tale Prologue to the Canterbury Tales
The Wife of Bath's Tale

Richard Church Over the Bridge

John Clare Selected Poetry and Prose

Samuel Taylor Coleridge Selected Poetry and Prose

Wilkie Collins The Woman in White

William Congreve The Way of the World

Joseph Conrad The Nigger of the Narcissus & Youth
The Secret Agent

Charles Dickens Bleak House David Copperfield Dombey and Son
Great Expectations Hard Times Little Dorrit Oliver Twist
Our Mutual Friend A Tale of Two Cities

Gerald Durrell My Family and Other Animals

George Eliot Middlemarch The Mill on the Floss Silas Marner

T. S. Eliot Murder in the Cathedral Selected Poems

J. G. Farrell The Siege of Krishnapur

Henry Fielding Joseph Andrews

F. Scott Fitzgerald The Great Gatsby

E. M. Forster Howards End A Passage to India
Where Angels Fear to Tread

William Golding Lord of the Flies The Spire

Oliver Goldsmith Two Plays of Goldsmith: She Stoops to Conquer;
The Good Natured Man

Graham Greene Brighton Rock The Power and the Glory
The Quiet American

Thom Gunn and Ted Hughes Selected Poems

Thomas Hardy Chosen Poems of Thomas Hardy
Far from the Madding Crowd Jude the Obscure
The Mayor of Casterbridge Return of the Native
Tess of the d'Urbervilles The Trumpet-Major

L. P. Hartley The Go-Between The Shrimp and the Anemone

Joseph Heller Catch-22

Ernest Hemingway For Whom the Bell Tolls
The Old Man and the Sea

Barry Hines A Kestrel for a Knave

Gerard Manley Hopkins Poetry and Prose of Gerard Manley Hopkins

Aldous Huxley Brave New World

Henry James Washington Square

Ben Jonson The Alchemist Volpone

James Joyce A Portrait of the Artist as a Young Man

John Keats Selected Poems and Letters of John Keats

Ken Kesey One Flew over the Cuckoo's Nest

Rudyard Kipling Kim

D. H. Lawrence The Rainbow Selected Tales Sons and Lovers

Harper Lee To Kill a Mockingbird

Laurie Lee As I Walked out One Midsummer Morning
Cider with Rosie

Thomas Mann Death in Venice & Tonio Kröger

Christopher Marlowe Doctor Faustus Edward the Second

W. Somerset Maugham Of Human Bondage

Gavin Maxwell Ring of Bright Water

Arthur Miller The Crucible Death of a Salesman

John Milton A Choice of Milton's Verse Comus and Samson
Agonistes Paradise Lost I, II

Sean O'Casey Juno and the Paycock
The Shadow of a Gunman and the Plough and the Stars

George Orwell Animal Farm 1984

John Osborne Luther

Alexander Pope Selected Poetry

J. B. Priestley An Inspector Calls

Siegfried Sassoon Memoirs of a Fox-Hunting Man

Peter Shaffer The Royal Hunt of the Sun

William Shakespeare Antony and Cleopatra As You Like It
Coriolanus Hamlet Henry IV (Part 1) Henry IV (Part 2) Henry V
Julius Caesar King Lear Love's Labour's Lost Macbeth Measure for
Measure The Merchant of Venice A Midsummer Night's Dream
Much Ado about Nothing Othello Richard II Richard III Romeo and
Juliet The Sonnets The Taming of the Shrew The Tempest Twelfth
Night The Winter's Tale

G. B. Shaw Androcles and the Lion Arms and the Man
Caesar and Cleopatra The Doctor's Dilemma Pygmalion Saint Joan

Richard Sheridan Plays of Sheridan: The Rivals; The Critic;
The School for Scandal

John Steinbeck The Grapes of Wrath Of Mice and Men & The Pearl

Tom Stoppard Rosencrantz and Guildenstern are Dead

J. M. Synge The Playboy of the Western World

Jonathan Swift Gulliver's Travels

Alfred Tennyson Selected Poetry

William Thackeray Vanity Fair

Flora Thompson Lark Rise to Candleford

Dylan Thomas Under Milk Wood

Anthony Trollope Barchester Towers

Mark Twain Huckleberry Finn

Keith Waterhouse Billy Liar

Evelyn Waugh Decline and Fall Scoop

H. G. Wells The History of Mr Polly The War of the Worlds

John Webster The White Devil

Oscar Wilde The Importance of Being Earnest

Virginia Woolf To the Lighthouse

William Wordsworth The Prelude (Books 1, 2)

John Wyndham The Chrysalids

W. B. Yeats Selected Poetry